Lionfishes and other Scorpionfishes

Aquarium Success

The complete guide to the successful care and breeding of these spectacular and popular marine fish

Frank C. Marini, Ph.D.

Dedicated to my parents, Frank Jr. and Rosemary, who set me on my path of curiosity and wonderment, and endowed me with the genetics to understand it all. I wouldn't be the same without them.

Lionfishes and Other Scorpionfishes

Project Team
Editor: David E. Boruchowitz
Indexer: Elizabeth Walker
Design: Patricia Escabi

T.F.H. Publications, Inc.
One TFH Plaza
Third and Union Avenues
Neptune City, NJ 07753

T.F.H. Publications
President/CEO: Glen S. Axelrod
Executive Vice President: Mark E. Johnson
Publisher: Christopher T. Reggio
Production Manager: Kathy Bontz

Printed and bound in China
10 11 12 13 14 1 3 5 7 9 8 6 4 2

Library of Congress Cataloging-in-Publication Data
Marini, Frank C.
  Lionfishes and other scorpionfishes : the complete guide to the successful care and breeding of these spectacular and popular marine fish / Frank C. Marini.
      p. cm.
  Includes index.
  ISBN 978-0-7938-1679-8 (alk. paper)
  1. Scorpionfishes. 2. Pterois. I. Title.
  SF458.S37M37 2010
  639.3'768--dc22
                    2010006683

This book has been published with the intent to provide accurate and authoritative information in regard to the subject matter within. While every reasonable precaution has been taken in preparation of this book, the author and publisher expressly disclaim responsibility for any errors, omissions, or adverse effects arising from the use or application of the information contained herein. The techniques and suggestions are used at the reader's discretion and are not to be considered a substitute for veterinary care. If you suspect a medical problem consult your veterinarian.

A Note on Measurements: When we convert between American and Metric System measurements, we use rounded-off conversions to provide equivalent levels of precision. Readers familiar with the mathematical concept of significant figures will recognize that these rounded conversions, while less precise, are actually more accurate because they are less precise. Where measurements are only approximate to begin with, as in the nominal gallonage of various standard aquarium sizes (where the actual volume is often quite different from the named size), we use only approximate, round conversions.

The Leader In Responsible Animal Care For Over 50 Years!®
www.tfh.com

Contents

Introduction

"What's that? I think it's looking at me."

My dad is pointing to this grayish lump on the bottom of a display at the Boston public aquarium. I scan all the identification cards surrounding the tank. I reply, pointing to a picture, "It's a skor-pin-a-day fish."

"You mean a scorpion, like the insect with a stinger?" my dad queries.

"Yeah, according to this, it pretends it's a rock and eats passing fish. It also carries poison and can kill a man if he steps on it."

Wow, I think…How cool is this?

Fast forward 30 years. I am a scientist by desire, training, and profession, but my fish hobbyist avocation predated my research training by many years. You might think that after all these years of keeping saltwater fish I've either personally experienced or read about just about anything that can occur. Well, I still learn new things daily. My tanks of scorpaeniform fish amaze me regularly.

You will notice a focus on lionfish in these pages. Although the book is a husbandry guide for all scorpaeniforms, lionfish are a prime example of the group. They're in every pet store, ogled by new aquarists wanting to get into saltwater aquariums. In my experience, if you get comfortable keeping lionfish, you'll have little issue keeping many of the other scorpions, as their requirements are very similar, and they can often be kept together. I'm hoping this book allows you to keep the fish of your dreams in the best possible environment you can provide. I hope this book fascinates you into pushing the envelope—maybe even breeding lionfish!

Scorpion Biology

Lions and triggers and eels…oh my! Nothing embodies the beauty and danger of the oceans more than lionfish. They're astonishingly beautiful, with gracefully flowing fins, dramatic colorations, cautious movements, and fish-gulping mouths. They're also equipped with venomous spines capable of delivering painful stings to an unwary hobbyist. In spite of all this, the lionfish and their bottom-crawling scorpionfish cousins are peaceful, extremely hardy, disease-resistant tank inhabitants that are well suited for the intermediate saltwater hobbyist.

Their hardiness, graceful movements, and stunning appearance have made lionfish extremely popular in the marine fish hobby—in spite of their venomous spines.

Nomenclature

The order Scorpaeniformes, the mail-cheeked fishes, contains the fishes known generally as scorpions and a host of other common names. Common names for fish are almost always imprecise and confusing, but the naming of the scorpaeniform fishes is particularly troublesome. Just a sampling of the common names used for various scorpaeniforms includes: butterfly cod, dragonfish, fan dancer, firefish, rockfish, scorpionfish, stinger, stingfish, stonefish, turkeyfish, upside-down flying cod, and zebrafish. Many of these names are used interchangeably to refer to a great number of species as well as to groups of species. This only gets more confusing when people use "lionfish" to refer to fishes in the subfamily Pteroinae of the family Scorpaenidae and "scorpionfish" to refer to fishes in the subfamily Scorpaeninae of the family Scorpaenidae.

To avoid confusion in this book, we'll follow two conventions. The first is a general convention used by biologists—we will use commonized forms of the names of scientific taxa to refer to the same fishes that the scientific names do. Thus, "scorpaeniforms" are fishes in the order Scorpaeniformes; "pteroines" are fishes in the subfamily Peteroinae; "scorpaenids" are fishes in the family Scorpaenidae; etc. Here is a list of the taxa we will be looking at, along with their commonized forms:

Order Scorpaeniformes: scorpaeniform
Family Scorpaenidae: scorpaenid
Family Synanceiidae: synanceiid
Family Tetrarogidae: tetrarogid
Subfamily Choridactylinae: choridactyline
Subfamily Pteroinae: pteroine
Subfamily Scorpaeninae: scorpaenine
Subfamily Synanceiinae: synanceiine

The second convention is that we will establish somewhat arbitrary definitions to keep things consistent while avoiding overuse of unwieldy taxonomic names. What follows is the biological classification of these fishes, with the terms in quotes being the common names we will use for the various groups. Just remember that we will stick to these definitions to avoid confusion in this book, but they will not necessarily apply elsewhere.

Order	Family	Subfamily	Arbitrary Name
Scorpaeniformes			"scorpions"
Scorpaeniformes	Scorpaenidae	Pteroinae	"lionfish"
Scorpaeniformes	Scorpaenidae	Scorpaeninae	"scorpionfish"
Scorpaeniformes	Synanceiidae	Choridactylinae	"stingfish" "sea goblins"
Scorpaeniformes	Synanceiidae	Synanceiinae	"stonefish"
Scorpaeniformes	Tetrarogidae		"waspfish"

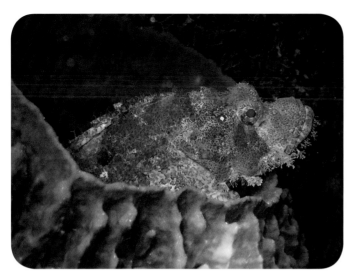

Scorpionfish are cryptic and sedentary relatives of the lionfish. This one is well camoflaged in a barrel sponge waiting for unsuspecting prey.

The order Scorpaeniformes includes 35 families, 300 genera, and more than 1400 species. Although most species are distributed throughout tropical and temperate marine waters, a few sculpins and the Australian bullrout have colonized fresh water. Many scorpaeniforms are well known for their venomous spines, but some play an important commercial role as protein-rich food stock for much of the world—these species are usually called rockfishes. Despite the danger the venomous rockfishes pose to divers and fishermen, they are among the most over-collected food fishes, representing more than 10 percent of the annual United States catch. This overfishing has resulted in the placement of four scorpaeniforms on the IUCN red list of endangered species and an additional 14 as vulnerable. If you enjoy dining on "Pacific snapper," which is not a snapper at all but a scorpaeniform, then you are acquainted with their moist white meat. Given the great diversity of this fish family, however, many of its members aren't commercially fished, although many of them figure prominently in the marine ornamental trade, collected only to populate our aquariums.

Beauty and the Beasts

The family Scorpaenidae comprises the subfamilies Pteroinae (the lionfishes) and Scorpaeninae (the scorpionfishes); some fishes of the families Tetrarogidae and Synanceiidae also are occasionally called scorpionfishes, but that is not the name we'll apply to them in this book. In appearance, the three families named here run the gamut—from the graceful flowing fins of the *Pterois* lion to the ghoulish, insect-headed *Choridactylus*, to the stonefish mimicking an algae-covered rock. If you love beautiful fishes, then these families will provide some for you. If you like your fishes to look unusual, weird, or hideous, they'll also give you many to fall in love with. Whether you enjoy a tank of swimming fishes or ground-crawling, substrate-digging ambush predators, you'll find a scorpion to fit into your tank, your heart, and—if you're like me—your head.

Most marine aquarists consider the very popular *Pterois volitans* lionfish as the ultimate lionfish, with the *Rhinopias* species as another Holy Grail. Although lionfishes have long been a mainstay at pet stores, others in the family are becoming more common. Don't overlook the hardiness of scorpaenids in captivity. Most of these fishes adapt well to aquarium life, eating pretty much anything and tolerating most tankmates—as long as they do not fit into their mouths, in which case they tolerate them on the inside.

Adult lionfishes are considered medium- to large-sized at 10 to 15 inches (25 to 40 cm) TL (total length) and should be housed in a fairly large aquarium of at least 100 gallons (400 liters).

Dwarf lions remain reasonably small at under 8 inches (20 cm) TL and can thrive in smaller tanks of 30 to 50 gallons (120 to 200 liters). Stonefishes are the largest of the other scorpions, but a few scorpions remain very manageable and work well in smaller tanks. Reef hobbyists are not precluded from scorpion options, since these fishes have no interest in sessile (non-moving) invertebrates. Though technically reef safe, they are of limited applicability to a reef aquarium. Besides their considerable waste output, they will chow down on such common reef tank specimens as peppermint shrimp and damselfishes.

Common names for the lionfishes vary, and one person's "turkeyfish" is someone else's "Russell's lion." I commonly see incorrect lionfish

Does Species Matter?

Proper identification of a fish by scientific name is extremely important for many reasons. In the aquarium trade, however, scientific names are often slapped on fish for sale without proper identification. With lionfish, however, it is fairly easy to distinguish the larger *Pterois* species from the dwarf *Dendrochirus* species. For the most part deciding the proper husbandry of these fishes doesn't require more identification than that. Whether a lionfish is identified only by a common name, by an incorrect scientific name, or by the right scientific name, you can enjoy it and provide the appropriate habitat.

Scorpionfish are masters of camouflage. Their coloration and dermal papillae allow them to perfectly blend in with their surroundings.

identifications at fish stores. Typically the large species are lumped together as "volitans lions" and the small species are all called just "dwarf lionfish." Fortunately, proper care of these animals is pretty much the same from species to species, so even if you buy a misidentified lionfish you should be able to keep it healthy and happy. You must, however, make sure you can identify it closely enough to know the approximate size it will reach. The biology of these fascinating fishes has a direct effect on their proper husbandry, so let's start with that.

Distribution and Habitat

Lionfishes and scorpionfishes are widespread in the world's oceans but are primarily found around coral reefs. Man has aided lionfish distribution over the past 50 years, with *Pterois miles* entering the Mediterranean Sea from the Red Sea via the Suez Canal. Also, *P. volitans* and *P. miles* were introduced into the Atlantic Ocean along the U.S. East Coast and have become established there. Scorpions are found in water depths ranging from 2 to 1260 feet (less than a meter to 380 meters), on hard and soft bottoms, coral reefs and artificial substrates (e.g., sunken ships or oil rigs). In corals reefs and rocky outcrops, the fish hide in caves and crevices and underneath rock overhangs. Many small scorpionfishes live among the coral rubble, while some larger forms lie in exposed areas waiting for passing food. Many species are well camouflaged, as they are replete with dermal appendages, muted color tones, and skin flaps and tassels that allow them to disappear from plain sight. A sedentary lifestyle enhances their ability to blend in and ambush unsuspecting passers-by.

Biological Features

Scorpaeniforms have many adaptations in anatomy and behavior that serve them well in the wild, adaptations that must be taken into account when keeping these animals in captivity.

Ecological Role

Easily outpaced by other animals, scorpionfish and lionfish are slow-moving hunters. Lionfish tend to appear conspicuous, so they rely on their unusual colorations and fins to discourage potential predators. On the reef, lionfish are top predators, as they are active hunters who ambush their prey using outstretched fins to slowly herd and corner their prey. As for scorpionfish, their strategy is different. They are extremely stealthy and sedentary, often sporting camouflaging coloration, feeding on prey that comes too close.

Behavior

Lionfish are active predators of smaller fish, crabs, and shrimp. They move by slowly undulating the soft rays of the dorsal and anal fins, stalking and cornering prey with outstretched, expanded pectoral fins. Their kill shot is a lightning-quick snap of the jaws, swallowing their prey whole in an instant. In the wild and in captivity, these fish

Lionfish, such as this beautiful *Pterois radiata*, use their outstretched pectoral fins to position prey where they can grab it with their expansive mouths.

can be cannibalistic. Lionfish appear mostly nocturnal, given their tendency to retreat to hiding areas during the day. However, in captivity we clearly observe lionfish feeding throughout the day, indicating that in the wild recently fed individuals may merely be retreating to their hiding spot after eating.

Most scorpionfish remain motionless for hours, relying on concealment to aid in ambushing their prey and feeding whenever the opportunity arises. On the reef, they feed on a few organisms a day, although large scorpionfish may ingest only one larger prey every few days. Scorpionfish diets vary, with some large scorpionfish feeding exclusively on fish. Others of similar size demonstrate a wide dietary breadth, feeding on shrimp, crabs, and squid in addition to fish. Many small scorpionfish feed almost exclusively on small crustaceans and worms. Like lionfish, scorpionfish tend to hunt mainly at twilight—they're crepuscular hunters—but they never pass up a meal opportunity, day or night.

Prey Capture The cavernous mouths of many scorpaeniform fishes are disproportionately large compared to their body size, so they are able to take even very large prey. Prey capture takes place in three phases: 1) orientation to the prey item, 2) seizing the prey (expansion and compression of the mouth) and 3) manipulating and swallowing the prey. When a scorpionfish sees a prey item, eye movements indicate the scorpionfish is tracking the prey. The scorpionfish raises its head slightly, visually orienting toward the prey's eyes. They attempt to orient their bodies toward the prey's head. This adjustment precedes the fish's rolling and pitching its pectoral fins to ensure the prey is within range.

Just before opening its mouth, the fish depresses its mouthparts, essentially spring-loading the mouth structures with potential energy to explode wide open for the strike. Bony fishes in general have similar mouth expansion biomechanics, but in scorpaeniforms mouth movement is so rapid that it creates a large lateral expansion, resulting in additional suction. The fish literally sucks the water surrounding the prey into its

Scorpionfish are ambush predators, able to remain motionless for hours until prey passes close enough to snap up.

mouth, rendering the prey as powerless to resist as a surfer on a bad wave. Once the prey is in its mouth, the fish holds it securely with its curved conical teeth, frequently manipulating the prey with abbreviated mouth expansion and closure—in essence, readjusting the food item to ensure it is head first. Swallowing occurs with a raking motion of the throat teeth. This entire process occurs swiftly— complete prey capture has been recorded at 45 milliseconds for a stonefish, with mouth opening and closing occurring in under 20 milliseconds (Grobecker, 1983).

The defensive posture of a bearded ghoul stingfish (*C. multibarbatus*). Note the erected dorsal spines and the outflared pec fins; this display is not a bluff—these fish have potently venomous spines.

Food Consumption and Starvation Only a small percentage of predatory fish have food in their stomachs when people catch them, compared to herbivorous fish whose stomachs are always full of plant material when captured. Researchers recently examined food consumption and ability to withstand starvation in two lionfish species (*Pterois volitans* and *Dendrochirus brachypterus*). Predatory fish must efficiently digest food when it's found. They then use these energy resources to stabilize themselves during fasting. Of the two species studied, *Dendrochirus* matured at 35 to 40 grams, and *Pterois* matured at 140 to 160 grams. Both species have parallel growth until they reach 30 grams, at which point *Pterois* grows exponentially. The researchers measured prey size and determined that *Pterois* requires 8.5 g/day for 14 months before reaching sexual maturity. On the other hand, *Dendrochirus* requires only 3.8 g/day for eight months, when it reaches 30 grams and becomes sexually mature.

The minimum food requirement for *Pterois* (8.5 g/day) translates to two or three small fish (3 to 5 grams), such as damsels or anthias. This doesn't mean you should restrict your fish's food—it just suggests that *Pterois* and *Dendrochirus* use food very efficiently, meaning they don't need to be fed much. Investigators also measured starvation effects on these well-fed fish and discovered *Pterois* lost only 22 percent of its body mass after 12 weeks of starving; during its 12-week fast, *Dendrochirus* lost 32 to 35 percent of its body mass, but only 12 percent at 2 weeks. These fish are obviously well equipped to survive for extended periods without food. (Fishelson, 1997)

Defensive Behavior Many scorpions rely on their cryptic coloration and sedentary nature to fend off predators. By being completely camouflaged, they rely on hiding in full view as a passive defense. Many have specialized body shapes and possess skin tassels that allow them to appear convincingly identical to algae tufts, rockpiles covered in sponges, or unpalatable crinoids. To supplement the camouflage, some scorpions mimic the undulating movement of local algae or debris; this is done, for example, by the leaf scorpions, whose bodies rock side-to-side, mimicking the wave action of local plants. However, if a predator stumbles across or threatens a scorpaeniform, the fish reacts. Initially it may flee, quickly settling into a new area, then quickly freezing again, remaining motionless. Alternatively, a few species possess brightly colored fin markings that are usually held in the closed, or darkened, position, such as on the bottom of the pectoral fin. These markings, called flashes or flasher fins, are rapidly exposed at a threat and may serve as a warning. Alternatively, the bright color flash may confuse or disorient predators.

Certain scorpaeniforms get their common names (stingfish, waspfish, etc.) from their ability to defend themselves with a venomous sting, although it's used as a last-resort defensive weapon to prevent a repeated attack. Venom glands at the base of certain spines produce a venom that the fish injects via the spines. The venom immediately causes severe pain that just about guarantees a hasty retreat of the threat. Medical and scientific journals have documented numerous cases of human envenomation, and I've dedicated a whole section to this topic later in this chapter.

Although they are mostly solitary fish, young lionfish sometimes form small groups. This probably provides the fish with some protection from predators.

Multifocal Lensed Eyes

Lionfish eyesight consists of a multifocal optical lens in each eye, with a short focal length (Karpstam, 2007). Long focal lengths equate to high optical magnification of the image and low light-gathering ability, meaning they can see farther but require hunting during daylight hours, whereas short focal lengths correspond with higher light-capturing ability and less magnification of the target, meaning more evening time hunting of prey that swims nearby. Because lionfish possess eyes better suited for their crepuscular behaviors, they strike at food from short distances and do more low-light hunting.

Dentition

Scorpaenids have many small teeth located on the upper and lower jaws in densely packed bilateral clusters, and in a small patch on the anterior roof of the mouth. These

An Ambon lionfish *(Pteroidichthys amboinensis)* shedding its cuticle. This is a normal occurence that allows the fish to get rid of external parasites.

small teeth appear functionally limited to grasping prey captured by the extraordinarily quick predatory strike. The pharyngeal (throat) teeth help them secure and swallow their meals.

Cuticle

Many scorpaeniforms lead an extremely sedentary lifestyle, and marine organisms (algae, hydroids, and bacteria that settle from the water column) can attach to them. Because of this, many have evolved a protective coating, called a cuticle. A cuticle is a thin white or opaque skin covering encasing the entire animal. The fish shed this cuticle to rid their bodies of these organisms. Some species, like *Rhinopias*, shed this cuticle weekly, and many others, such as lionfish, shed monthly or even less frequently. Shedding can take minutes to hours. Shedders shake their body rapidly until the cuticle tears off in small pieces. In home aquariums, cuticle shedding looks unsettling. In a lionfish, you'll notice that the fish darts and dives, then convulses for a few seconds; a white, ghost-like tissue appears in the water. The cuticle protects the fish from illness, and excessive cuticle shedding indicates poor health, as they increase cuticle shedding during protozoan infection as a way of reducing their exposure.

Predators

Few published records of natural predators of scorpionfish and lionfish exist. One short report suggests that the piscivorous cornetfish *Fistularia commersoni* is a predator of *Pterois miles*. Judging by the presence and reverse orientation of a partially digested specimen of *P. miles* in the stomach of a large *F. commersoni*, the authors concluded that cornetfish may ambush lionfish from the rear, consuming them tail-first, allowing the venomous spines to fold harmlessly forward. In the home aquarium, venomous spines aren't a deterrent to larger piscivores, as I've personally witnessed antennariids (frogfish and anglerfish) consume small lionfish. Additionally, other scorpions readily consume smaller ones. I have watched in horror as my large *P. volitans* engulfed two juvenile conspecifics. It is likely that natural lionfish predators include sharks, as many sharks consume noxious organisms without displaying ill effects from the poisons.

Social Structure

Lionfish are often seen moving about during the day, alone and in groups of two to six animals. They may live alone most of their lives, fiercely defending their home ranges from other lionfish. As juveniles, lionfish aggregate into small groups, and this cooperation probably increases their ability to gather food. During the spawning season, adult lionfish also may gather into groups, with males acting more aggressively than females. In many lionfish no clear sexual dimorphism or dichromatism exists— however, clear demarcation between sexes exists in *Dendrochirus brachypterus*, the dwarf fuzzy lionfish. Lionfish reproduce like many other fish, producing eggs that are fertilized outside the female's body. There is little information about the social structure of most reef-dwelling scorpionfish species. Most observations about these fishes are from anecdotal reports from scuba divers and aquarists keeping them.. We do know that most tropical species remain solitary, with occasional sightings of scorpionfish pairs, and the leaf scorpionfish have been noted in pairs and trios.

The relationships between scorpaeniform fishes are not well understood. For example, in the scorpionfish genus *Rhinopias*, some fish appear to be intermediate or transitional forms between the two recognized species *R. frondosa* (above left) and *R. eschmeyeri* (above right), a possible indication these are not separate species. Using key characteristics which define the species, you'll notice that the fish to the left has an occellate patterning and window pane-like pectoral fins, both features for *R. frondosa*. However it possess mustache-like extensions and has no subocular projections which are characteristics of *R. eschmeyeri*.

A Taxonomy in Turmoil

Cuvier erected Scorpaeniformes in 1829, describing the taxon based on the observation that members shared "a posterior extension of the third circumorbital that reaches back across the periopercle." This characteristic, known as the suborbital stay or mail-cheek spine, has single-handedly held this order together for nearly 200 years. Recently taxonomists have tried to unite the Scorpaeniformes by using meristic and morphological observations about parietal lateral lines, length of dorsal spines, shape of dermal appendages, etc., but none of it has been any more successful than using the presence of the mail-cheek spine.

In 2002 molecular biologists began applying DNA analysis to these fishes, starting to throw scorpaeniform intrarelationships into confusion. Physical descriptions identify the common cheek-spine, but DNA fragments linking mitochondrial and nuclear sequence relationships from founder populations to the present fishes have resulted in a murky species diagram (Smith, WL, 2004). In the past 15 years, no fewer than five attempts to reclassify and reorganize the Scorpaenidae have failed (Imamura, 1998, 2002, Shinohara, 1994). These problems do not affect us hobbyists very much. The fishes are still the same fishes; they just might be called something else a few years from now.

Atlantic Lionfish?

Widely distributed throughout the western Pacific Ocean from southern Japan to Micronesia and Australia to the Philippines, both *Pterois volitans* and *P. miles* cover a good portion of the Pacific Ocean. However, more than 15 years ago (in 1992), a few western Pacific lionfish were observed by divers off Boca Raton and Palm Beach, Florida. In 1995, one lionfish was caught by a fisherman in waters off Jacksonville, Florida, and in 2001 reports appeared that numerous individuals were observed by scuba divers off the coasts of North Carolina. Since 2001, individuals and groups of lionfish are being reported along the eastern seaboard, as far north as New Jersey and Long Island, New York, and individual fish have been reported as far south as Cuba and as far east as Bermuda.

So how can a tropical fish like a lionfish, found across a different ocean, end up as an invasive species off the US coast? Many theories exist, and they include both accidental and intentional release of aquarium specimens. Some conclude that the lionfish invasion originated in Florida, where adults bred and pelagic eggs were carried north by the water currents. The northern boundary for overwintering was believed to be Cape Hatteras, North Carolina because lionfish were thought to perish at water temperatures below 60°F (16°C). Juvenile fish transported through the Gulf Stream as far north as New York during the warmer seasons and were thought to die off during the winter. This appears not to be the case. Over the past seven years numerous studies have been conducted demonstrating a steady increase in the population of lionfish. In November 2008, lionfish densities off the southwest coast of New Providence, Bahamas recorded the highest densities yet described: approximately 390 lionfish per hectare. As a comparison, in their native ocean *P. volitans* lionfish are found at a density of 80 lionfish per hectare (Green, 2008). Given the high density of these lionfish, many researchers are concerned about the negative impact they will have on local populations of coral-reef and game fishes that they prey on.

Some lionfish, such as *P. mombassa,* have bold eye spots on their pectoral fins that may serve to startle or disorient prey items when the fish flare their fins

Fins: Beautiful but Deadly

We'll end our discussion of scorpaeniform biology with a look at one of the group's more remarkable features: the fins.

Pectoral Prowess

Lionfish are hunters and ambush predators, and their pectoral fins make them well adapted to the role. These fins are flamboyant, colorful, and very mobile. When a lionfish stalks its prey, it uses the pectoral fins to perform a number of tasks, often swaying them from side to side and slightly forward, an action that seems to make the fish's approach less disturbing to the intended victim. Additionally, by tilting the fins forward, the lionfish creates a barrier or fencing and uses it to herd the prey to a certain spot, restricting its movement.

As the lionfish moves in closer, preparing to swallow the food item, the pectoral fins are frequently tilted and shaken (most likely to distract the prey and, just as importantly, to allow the lionfish to focus on the eye of the food animal). Large volitans lions will often drag their pectoral fins across the substrate to flush out any hiding prey. Similarly, in the dwarf lionfish species, the fin movements are frequently exaggerated when hunting. Dwarf fuzzy lionfish twitch their dorsal and pectoral spines when hunting. Fu Man Chu lionfish, *D. biocellatus,* have a unique rhythmic, sequential back-and-forth twitching of their dorsal spines, and they vibrate only the ray tips of their pectoral fins when hunting prey items. The dorsal spine movements are thought to distract and confuse prey and enhance the lionfish's hunting ability.

Most lionfish are brightly colored under the lighting of the home aquarium, but in low-light situations, like those found at dusk and dawn, the brightly colored markings become dark disruptive patterns that serve as a camouflage, making a lionfish less visible to potential prey. The pectoral fins also serve another purpose: when threatened by a predator, a lionfish will spread these fins widely, orient its head facing down to aim its venomous spines forward, and present a formidable and menacing target to the attacker. In a few lionfish species, the inner pectoral fins have boldly marked eyespots and, when displayed, these eyespots may scare off or confuse potential predators.

Scorpionfish Pectorals

The pectoral fins are also very important to the more bottom-hugging scorpaeniform fishes. They use their pectoral fins to maintain posture, and many species rest on their pectoral fins. By moving side to side on the erected fins a fish can slowly move or crutch its way stealthily across the ocean bottom.

Additionally, a few species of scorpions, such as *Scorpaena plumieri*, keep their pectoral fins close to the body in a folded state, but when the fish is threatened the pectoral fin is held reversed, with the axillary surface now exposed—resulting in a bright yellow flash of color. This color marking is also seen in *Inimicus* and *Choridactylus* species that rapidly open and close their pectoral fins to serve as a warning. Speaking of these two genera, these fish have developed a unique mode of locomotion that relies on two or three free pectoral fin rays that are not connected to the fins by a membrane. These fin rays are moved independently like fingers to walk across the substrate, and are also used to dig and stir up buried prey items.

Aquatic Ballet

The graceful movements of a lionfish are often compared to ballet, and although the purposes of the fish's behavior are usually territorial or predatory rather than artistic, you can enjoy the show all the same. Since lionfish are also intelligent and curious, they often interact with their keepers through the glass, showing real interest in what's going on outside the tank and perhaps even displaying just for you.

Venom

More than 200 species of marine fishes, including lionfishes, scorpionfishes, stonefishes, stingrays, toadfishes, weevers, stargazers, surgeonfishes, and blennies, have been found to be venomous (Russell, 1996). Most of these are sedentary predators found in relativity shallow waters (Maretic, 1988), and scientific theories link sedentary fish with the evolution of a venom apparatus for protective purposes (Cameron, 1973). Although only a handful of species of venomous fish possess the ability to cause human mortality, many of these species can produce severe envenomation.

Delivering the Venom We can subdivide Scorpaeniformes into three groups based on the structure of the venom organs, ranging from the most primitive in lionfish to

Therapy

intermediate structure in the scorpionfish and finally to the most developed in stonefish. The venom appears similar among all three groups, although potency differs. Lionfish venom is the least potent, with the deadly stonefish's venom similar in potency to cobra venom.

While the sting of most species is not considered life-threatening, it is very painful and causes symptoms such as extremely low blood pressure and cellulitis. Their venoms contain many pharmacologically active components. To be classified as venomous, a fish must not only secrete a noxious substance from specialized glands but also possess some form of specialized delivery apparatus (envision a hypodermic needle). In some species, for example the stonefish, *Synanceia* spp., which are deadly scorpaeniforms, these venomous spines are highly developed, with distinct venom glands and ducts associated with the spine. In other species the venom apparatus is less developed, being composed of a spine somewhat loosely associated with the venomous products. The envenomating apparatus of the lionfish *P volitans* consists of 12 or 13 (out of 18) dorsal spines, two pelvic spines, and three anal spines, all associated with venom glands. The pectoral spines are not associated with venom glands.

No matter how developed, the delivery apparatus of all venomous fishes consists of the same basic structure—a spine associated with venom-secreting cells, all covered in a protective integumentary (skin-like) sheath. Venom is expressed when the spine enters the tissue of the victim, the sheath encasing the spine is ruptured, and the venom flows into the wound.

Pharmacological Effects of Fish Venoms A variety of toxins have been isolated from the venoms of fishes, and in general toxic proteins possess all of the lethal activity and usually are responsible for a number of the other biological activities. In contrast to terrestrial animals, such as snakes and arachnids, fish venoms appear to contain only a few toxins; however, to supplement the potency of the toxin, fish venoms contain other biologically active components that exacerbate the pain and physiological response

(Khoo, HE, 2002).

All venomous fish use their venom primarily for defensive purposes, and all fish venoms produce a similar set of symptoms, in particular extreme pain. Another very important characteristic shared by many fish venoms, and one that has

Close-up view of the venomous spines along the back of a stingfish (*Inimicus didactylus*).

hindered scientific research on studying these venoms, is that they are compositionally labile—meaning they decompose readily when exposed to certain ranges of temperature and pH. People who are stung can exploit this by using heat to relieve the symptoms of a sting. While there is debate as to whether heat actually breaks down the venom or is just relieving the physical symptoms (Fenner PJ, 2000), clear evidence shows that immersing the envenomated body part (usually the hand or fingers) in hot water alleviates the symptoms of the venom of most species (Wasserman GS,1979, Patel MR, 1993, Chan TY, 1996, Sutherland, 2001).

A major concern of hobbyists concerning stings from a fish is their lethality, but the evidence indicates that stings from lionfish and the majority of scorpionfish are very painful but not fatal. This does not apply to stonefish stings, which definitely are extremely dangerous. In a recent study, no fatalities were reported out of 404 persons treated at emergency rooms for scorpaenid envenomation (Schaper, 2008). These data support earlier studies (Vetrano, 2002), (Garyfallou, 1996), and (Keizer, 1985) that demonstrate out of 163 emergency room visits for lionfish envenomation, no fatalities were reported. Of course, as with any exposure to antigens, including a bee sting, there is the possibility of individual sensitivity and death from anaphylactic shock if untreated, so it is vital to seek medical attention, especially if there is any nausea, difficulty in breathing, or other symptoms not specifically related to the envenomation site.

Do you see the stonefish? Its camouflage is perfect, and it is an interesting animal, but stonefish are dangerously venomous and should not be kept by marine hobbyists.

Getting Stung—It Can Happen to You

All the fishes covered in this book possess venom glands in their dorsal, anal, and pelvic spines. The primary function of these spines is a defensive measure against threats and predators. The amount of venom injected from each spine is dependent on how much pressure is being placed on the spine and the amount of time the spine is left in the tissue. In the home aquarium stings are very rare but do occur.

For example, when you are maneuvering or transferring a lionfish it will often be exposed and may thrash around in defense, with an inadvertent sting as a result. While the lionfish won't rush towards you or race across the aquarium when you are maintaining it, the act of putting your hands into the lionfish's environment serves to put it on alert. It might hide under the very rockwork being rearranged or against the glass being cleaned. It may also think you are introducing food and hover nearby. If your movements inadvertently trap or corner a lionfish it will become defensive and raise its spines.

One day I was cleaning my tank, vacuuming the substrate, moving the rockwork around. All my lionfishes (and scorpionfishes), are trained to take silversides and meat strips when I wiggle the food in front of them, so I assume a few of the fishes were coming over to consider whether my fingers were food. I initially just shooed them away, but one of them was persistent and kept coming back. At one point, I was contemplating where to place the next rock and not really paying attention to the task, but my hand and arm were submerged, and I felt something brush my arm. Reflexively, I jerked my hand back, and this sudden movement spooked the lion sufficiently for him to immediately point head down with his dorsal spines extended. I impaled myself onto an outstretched spine. I immediately pulled my hand out, looked at where the spine had entered—no blood—and continued cleaning the tank. After about 30 seconds my hand started throbbing up to my wrist. At first, it was like a bee sting in intensity, and the pain increased. After five minutes it felt like a bee sting on steroids!

This happened back in 1990, when there was little, if any, knowledge on what to do for a lionfish envenomation. I rushed to the emergency room (concerned mainly by what I had read online about lionfish stings and their venom). I was very scared, and what made matters worse was that the doctor had never heard of a lionfish or a scorpionfish! Since the physician had little idea what to do, he treated the wound like a wasp sting. He rubbed the area with a strong corticosteroid solution and put me on a strong antihistamine. The pain lasted for about a half hour more; my hand throbbed and ached, even burned at times. My hand suffered from numb areas for three days after this event. Unfortunately, I have been stung two more times since then, and each time it was 100 percent my fault. I've learned that just reaching into the tank and grabbing an overturned rock could yield a hiding lionfish. I can tell you from experience that you don't want this to happen twice in your lifetime, and you definitely don't want it to happen three times! So my advice is: don't get stung! Pay ultimate respect to these fishes at all times, and whenever you perform any task in your tank, know where a lionfish is at all times and be wary of it; even better, place a plastic divider between you and the fish.

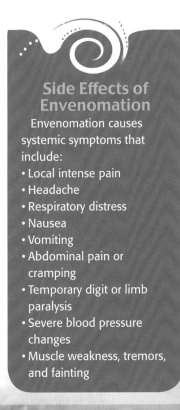

Side Effects of Envenomation

Envenomation causes systemic symptoms that include:
- Local intense pain
- Headache
- Respiratory distress
- Nausea
- Vomiting
- Abdominal pain or cramping
- Temporary digit or limb paralysis
- Severe blood pressure changes
- Muscle weakness, tremors, and fainting

A Home Aquarium for Lionfish and Scorpionfish

This book assumes a moderate level of experience as a marine aquarist, so I will simply remind you of some aspects of husbandry and note where scorpaenids have special requirements. I've been in the hobby long enough to know that no particular approach is right or wrong. If it works for you, it's correct; if it doesn't, change it. The good news about scorpaenids is that they are hardy, tolerant fish that eat well and thrive wonderfully in captivity. They really do make good aquarium specimens, and if you're into fish that recognize you and interact with you, consider getting some *Dendrochirus* lionfish. It will make your day.

It is best to use the largest tank your space and budget will allow. For a large lionfish, such as this *P. volitans*, consider a 100-gallon (400-liter) aquarium to be the minimum size.

The Tank

The best advice is to purchase the largest tank you can afford that will fit into your available space. There are countless stories of people starting out in their fishy endeavors with a small fish tank only to find within a very short time that they wish they had purchased a much larger tank, but I've never heard of someone lamenting that they bought too large a tank!

Make It Big

Aside from the issue of sufficient space so the fish are not cramped, larger water volumes are much more stable; temperatures rise and fall more slowly, and water quality issues take longer to develop, affording you time to correct any problems.

For large-bodied lionfish consider nothing smaller than a 100-gallon (400-liter) tank;

a 200-gallon (800-liter) or larger is even better. An adult *Pterois* has a wide pectoral fin spread, and the fish must have an aquarium with an 18-inch (46-cm) or larger width so it can turn around without having to fold back its fins. For midsized lions consider no less than a 75-gallon (300-liter) tank.

For those interested in scorpionfishes, which tend to be smaller than the lionfishes, consider a 30-gallon (110-liter) tank a minimum. I've seen a number of hobbyists display their *Rhinopias* and other scorpionfishes in long tanks that were subdivided using baffles; this way a lot of water can hold many beautiful fishes without their having access to one another. This is a nice alternative to having many smaller tanks in which water quality might quickly become an issue. No fish in this group is suitable for a nano tank.

Sump/Refugium

A sump is an additional container plumbed directly into the main tank wherein you can place filtration equipment, perform various maintenance tasks, and increase your total water volume without having a bigger display tank. A refugium is a sump that is used to provide refuge, usually for plants and animals that would be eaten up in the main aquarium. Refugia are usually filled with various species of algae, a sand or mud bed, and live rock; hence they provide additional filtration as well. There are numerous benefits to having a sump, such as having a hidden area to place your skimmer, bio-media, and wet/dry filter or a place to dose your supplements and top off water without getting your hands into the display tank. Do you need a sump? No, but in my experience a sump is well worth having.

Example of a refugium that hangs on the back of the tank. This one houses some caulerpa algae and a baby waspfish.

Lighting

There are many variations of lighting for marine tanks. Keeping scorpions lends itself to very simple lighting, as all you really need is enough light for the fish to see their food and for you to enjoy them. In fact, most cryptic scorpionfish and dawn-and-dusk hunters like lionfish appreciate dimmer lighting. However, if you have a reef tank with high-intensity lighting. you must ensure you provide dark hiding spots or caves in your tank to accommodate your fish's desire to hide in the dark.

Filtration

Inadequate filtration and poor water quality are behind most of the problems that occur in marine aquariums. This is especially so when keeping piscivorous fish, which eat meaty foods and produce lots of nitrogenous waste. Their wastes can quickly overwhelm and pollute even a large tank if there isn't adequate filtration.

Biological Filtration (Biofiltration)

Biological filtration refers to living components within your tank that assist in the breakdown of organic pollutants. Many of these breakdown organisms (primarily bacteria) are critical to the nitrogen cycle and convert toxic ammonia into relatively harmless nitrate. These creatures are found as biofilms that coat your substrates, tank walls, filter media, and the pores of live rock. Essentially every surface that is in contact with water from your tank can provide surface area for biofiltration. However, some areas are much better than others at providing sufficient water movement,

Easy Lighting

The easiest route to go for fish-only tank lighting is a premanufactured lighting hood with single or double fluorescent tubes. Buy it, add the light bulbs, set it on your tank and plug it in. Over the years I've found using a timer also makes life easier. My personal choice has been to see my fish when I get home from work; therefore, I have my lighting come on from 5:00 to 11:00 pm. During the day, ambient room light is sufficient, my fish know when I'm coming to feed them, and they honestly don't seem fazed by not having more light.

Live rock provides lots of surface area for biological filtration. It's also used by fish—*Scorpaenodes littoralis* in this photo—for hiding, foraging, and marking territory.

oxygen levels, and access to nutrients. Filters that provide biofiltration are designed to maximize the growth and health of these bacterial colonies and include such things as wet/dry, fluidized sand bed, and canister filters, as well as deep sand beds and live rock, both in the aquarium and in a refugium.

The key here is patience; these bacterial colonies take time to mature into a functional filter. This process is called cycling an aquarium, and a discussion of cycling is outside the scope of this book. You must make sure you are familiar with the subject and know how to properly cycle your tank before you purchase any fish for it. This is true for any aquarium and for any type of fish. In the marine hobby today many people rely heavily on live rock for cycling, and you will find plenty of information about how to do this.

Chemical Filtration

Chemical filtration chemically alters, sequesters, or removes harmful substances. The most utilized chemical medium is activated carbon.

Activated Carbon Granulated activated carbon (GAC) is carbon that has been exposed to high temperature and pressures. This process drives out any gases and impurities, leaving behind extremely porous and purified chips of carbon. This porous structure within the carbon chips creates a gigantic sponge that can remove many water impurities by trapping them (absorption) or by chemically attracting them (adsorption).

One of the most common discussions about the use of carbon is how much to use and how often to replace it. Since no two tank setups are identical, this is a difficult question to answer. You should experiment to find out how much you need.

Lionfish, like this *Dendrochirus brachypturus*, produce large amounts of waste and truely benefit from excellent filtration.

Start by adding 8 ounces of GAC for each 50 gallons (1.2 g per liter) of tank water. GAC will remove yellowing dissolved organic compounds (DOC) from your water and make it look clear. Hold a sheet of white paper behind the tank and look at it through the water; this will reveal whether the water is yellow. If your tank water doesn't clear after adding GAC, add more. You can then replace the carbon after your tank water starts to yellow again. While this is not very precise, you can use it as a rough indicator.

GAC is extremely porous and will quickly be covered by a biofilm of bacteria, creating a good biofilter but a poorer chemical medium. Also, as GAC ages some of the substances it has removed can be released back into your water, so be diligent in your replacement schedule. I find that an old knee-high nylon stocking makes a great GAC bag. I keep two on hand—one in use in the tank and one ready to go after the exchange. Always place GAC in the water flow where water has to pass thru the GAC and cannot bypass it.

Other Media Another useful chemical filtrant is a molecular absorption medium. This is a porous filter medium impregnated with various styrene or acrylic polymers that selectively adsorb polar organics and nitrogen-containing compounds onto their surfaces. This filter pad can substitute for GAC, but importantly it removes many more dissolved organics and heavy metals; it even binds nitrate. I find it very useful in removing residual antibiotics and copper-based treatments, and I use it after a tank crash when an unknown pollutant has contaminated my tank.

Not a Cure-All At this point I would like to clarify that chemical filtration is *not* a replacement for water changes. No method of chemical filtration is 100 percent efficient, and many substances are quite difficult to bind chemically. What chemical filtration will do for your tank is allow you to maintain a lower concentration of dissolved organics, but you still need to do water changes and perform other regular maintenance. And, of course, chemical filtration cannot replace depleted substances—another important function of water changes.

Mechanical Filtration

Mechanical filtration physically removes particulate waste from the water. This filtration frequently comes in the form of foam pads, sponges, dense fiber inserts, and filter bags that are placed into the water flow and trap the organic matter suspended in the water. Always use coarse filter material first in line, at the water interface, to filter large debris, followed by finer media to capture the small particles. While I highly recommend the use of mechanical filtration in keeping scorpions, these filters require the most upkeep. Since these filters trap waste, they become clogged and must be cleaned or replaced frequently. In fact, they need frequent cleaning even if they aren't clogged, since the wastes trapped in the media continue to decompose and add to the dissolved pollutants. Replacing or cleaning the debris-filled filter media once a week will go a long way toward maintaining water quality.

Tides

Remember going to the beach and enjoying the ebb and flow of the tide coming in and the undertow pulling you back out, just watching your foot get buried in the loose sand? Relaxing, isn't it? The push and pull of tides is what exchanges water, providing fresh oxygen and nourishment and removing waste. This effect is frequently even more pronounced in lagoons and along coastal waters where the change of tides is accompanied with strong currents and undertows. This is how we need to think as hobbyists to ensure the best water quality for our fish.

Skimming

The protein skimmer originated in the wastewater treatment industry many years ago. It was used primarily to reduce the organic load before the water reached the activated sludge reactors. This technique exploits the affinity of organic waste to adsorb to air bubbles. In basic terms, organic-waste-laden aquarium water is reacted in a column of air bubbles, creating foam. The waste sticks in the foam. The foam gets thicker as the individual bubbles stick together, and as they coalesce and dry the foam bubbles over the top and into the collector. Of the various filtration methods we discussed, only foam fractionation completely removes most organics before they begin to break down in waste.

Working Together

The benefits of biological, chemical, and mechanical filtration synergize into a complete working system that keeps your aquarium water as healthy and clear as possible. Almost all filtration systems will utilize mechanical and biological filtration, and most of them will allow you to add chemical filtration. Choosing the right filtration system for your aquarium usually depends on the size of the aquarium, your specific filtration requirements, and your budget. In small tanks, hang-on-the-back filters and smaller hang-on-tank or in-tank skimmers are very appropriate, whereas a 300-gallon (1100-liter) display tank full of lionfish will require a much more extensive and costly filter setup. There is no single right way or only way to accomplish this task, and many different systems can get the job done.

Because of the importance of your filtration system in the overall health and performance of your tank, I highly suggest you consult other hobbyists, reputable fish shop owners, and online resources to research what is available. That way you can make informed aquarium filtration purchases.

There are some water quality technologies that don't fit well into the simple triad of biological, chemical, and mechanical filtration. Certainly the most important of these is protein skimming, also known as foam fractionation.

Skimmers

Although popularly called "protein skimmers," these devices remove a great variety of dissolved substances from the water that passes through them. They are so effective in maintaining water quality that many aquarists who otherwise rely on live rock alone for filtration also utilize a skimmer. You shouldn't even consider leaving one out of your lionfish or scorpionfish system.

A great deal of the unwanted organic wastes dissolved in aquarium water are surfactants (surface-active materials) that collect at a gas-liquid interface. These surfactants come from many sources, including fish wastes, uneaten food, and decomposing matter. The protein skimmer originated in the wastewater treatment industry many years ago and was used to reduce the organic load before the water reached the activated sludge reactors, but it performs the same duty in the marine aquarium. Unlike many other filtration methods, foam fractionation completely removes dissolved organics from the system before they begin to break down. In my opinion a skimmer is an indispensable piece of equipment for keeping scorpion/lionfish—or any other fish, really. After you see firsthand the amount of skimmate removed from your tank and how nasty the dark liquid looks and smells, you'll know why every marine tank needs a skimmer. There is a great variety in skimmer design, and they vary greatly

Most scorpaeniforms, like this spectacular red leaf fish (*Taenianotus triacanthus*), require aquarium temperatures that stay between 70° and 80°F (21° and 26°C). A red leaf fish is shown

in efficiency. Get your dealer to describe the various models and pick one rated for a larger tank than you actually have. A good skimmer costs money and is one piece of equipment you shouldn't skimp on or have to buy twice.

Heaters/Chillers

While the seas around tropical reefs do not fluctuate very much in daily or yearly temperatures, aquariums can experience wide variations in temperatures. Heaters and chillers are necessary to stabilize your aquatic environment. Unless the room in which your aquarium is situated stays between 70° and 80°F (21° and 26°C), you will definitely need equipment to regulate the temperature. Even within that range, you will need to stabilize the water temperature if there are rapid swings in room temperature.

Heaters

For larger tanks, such as you will need to keep scorpaeniforms of any kind, figure on two to three watts per gallon (0.5 to 1 watt per liter) to determine the size of the heater you need. It's a good idea to divide that number by 2 or 3 and purchase two or three heaters that add up to the total wattage—if one stops heating the tank won't cool off too fast, and if one should fail in the on position, it won't be powerful enough to overheat your tank and cook your occupants before you discover the problem.

Chillers

Chillers clearly serve their purpose for those who live in very warm climates, and for the advanced hobbyist willing to try to keep a temperate fish like the bluefin lionfish, *Parapterois, which* requires water of 62° to 65°F (16° to 18°C). The drawbacks of chillers are the same as any other compressor-based cooling technology and include that they can be noisy, they use a lot electricity, and they generate large amounts of waste heat.

Water Flow and Aeration

Water in the ocean is in a perpetual state of motion, and it is important to replicate this environment in our aquariums. Water flow in your aquarium helps to evenly distribute dissolved gases and to encourage gas exchange (oxygen in, carbon dioxide out). Most gas exchange occurs at the surface of your tank; if your tank were to be stagnant, surface films would reduce the exchange of gases. In addition, moving water effectively renews the surface constantly, bringing all the water in the tank for a pass by the surface. Wet/dry filters and skimmers also boost oxygen levels considerably. In addition to gas exchange, water movement prevents dead areas from forming, forcing any detritus into the water column, where it will be removed by the filtration system. You should make sure that there is enough current so that debris is not able to settle on the bottom.

Water movement can be created through the use

Bluefin lionfish (*Parapterois heterura*) are unusual lionfish in several ways, including that they prefer temperate water temperatures instead of tropical ones.

of filtration pumps and returns, closed-loop systems, and powerheads. In a small aquarium water movement from the hang-on-back filter and an additional powerhead is fine. For larger tanks adding powerheads at opposite sides of the tank will ensure proper flow. In tanks of 100 gallons (400 liters) or more, the use of closed-loop systems, multiple powerheads, and combinations of return pumps will be needed to provide sufficient water movement within the tank.

Water Changes

While all this filtration is a great thing, nothing can compare to refreshing the quality of your water with good water changes. By changing as little as 15 to 20 percent weekly (30 percent in larger tanks) you can rejuvenate the quality of your water, add fresh micronutrients, and dilute any pollution.

When doing water changes, you must match the temperature, salinity, and buffering of the replacement water to the tank water. I do my water changes as part of my twice-monthly tank maintenance. I usually exchange 50 gallons (190 liters) the first change and 30 gallons (115 liters) during the second change in my 180-gallon (690-liter) tank.

Siphoning

I've talked with many hobbyists who after performing a water change have reported to me that they have crashed their biofilter or created a cloudy tank, and their animals are suffering. With this in mind, I'll provide a primer on correct siphoning.

Waste products, such as detritus, fish poop, and even heavier dissolved molecules, can sink to the bottom of your tank and accumulate. Therefore the lower regions of your tank are dirtier than the upper zones. Detritus can also settle into your substrate. Obviously, you should place your siphon at the lowest regions of your tank and draw off the water from there.

If you have a simple crushed coral substrate, use a gravel tube—a substrate-cleaning siphon attachment. Clean only half of the tank bottom during each cleaning. Do this by sticking the gravel tube into the crushed coral, allowing the dark gunk to run up the siphon while the heavier substrate grains fall back down. When the water runs clear, move the gravel tube to another spot and repeat until you have covered half the substrate. If you use a live sand bed, place the siphon as close to the sand as possible and allow the vortex suction to lift any detritus and gunk upward. In this case you should not clean the sandbed, since it functions by stratifying different zones of oxygen levels, and stirring them disrupts the strata. In a bare-bottom tank you can safely siphon the whole bottom during each cleaning.

By removing the wastes accumulated at the bottom of your tank, you'll be changing the water most effectively by removing much of the dirt. By leaving half of the substrate untouched, you'll be leaving the biofilter only minimally disturbed. Any bacterial colonies removed by siphoning the substrate will quickly recolonize while the undisturbed half continues to function at full efficiency.

Aquascaping

Dressing up your tank taps into your creative side as well as motivates you to recreate a natural environment for your fish. You'll want to design an environment that is both beneficial to your tank residents and that is aesthetically pleasing for you. Over the years I've seen totally empty tanks loaded with fish that were beautiful because they showcased the fish, but I can only imagine that the fish seemed bored just swimming around and not interacting with their environment.

In this regard many hobbyists have gone to a concept of fish only with live rock (FOWLR) tanks. In a FOWLR tank pieces of live rock are placed in the tank, not only to act as biofilters but also to provide a natural environment for the fishes to interact with, hide in,

Even with excellent filtration, you will need to perform regular water changes to keep your lionfish's water in top condition. Shown here is a baby volitans lion.

and crawl upon. To me it just makes sense to re-create some of the natural surrounding the fish live in and clearly feel more at ease in. If you do use live rock (and I recommend you do) as your primary filtration medium, then a minimum of 1 to 2 pounds per gallon (0.1 to 0.2 kg per liter) will be required. If you use a live sand bed you can use less live rock.

Even if you only plan on the rock to provide supplemental filtration, it can be very decorative. I've seen beautiful setups with two live rock piles at opposite ends; I've seen cave structures and rock walls that would rival the Roman Colosseum. My personal choice is to provide the fish with sufficient caves and hiding places to feel comfortable. I don't stack piles of rock up too high, and I try to provide open spaces on the substrate for the scorpionfish to crawl around.

If you plan on keeping large-bodied lionfish, you should provide them with more swimming space, but in general a good mix of open substrate and swimming space with hiding places will allow you to keep a variety of species in the aquarium.

Some hobbyists try to re-create specific ocean or lagoon biotopes, and this is an excellent idea. Finding out where a fish is from and trying to provide it with a small slice of its home is a very appealing concept. Many scuba diving websites are filled

When aquascaping your tank, remember that most scorpaeniforms, such as *Scorpaenodes littoralis*, need caves and other hiding places.

with underwater photos of tropical destinations, and these websites are an excellent place to start your research. On the other hand, some hobbyists take a less natural approach, and in this regard I've seen the use of artificial corals, bleached coral skeletons, plastic plants, live marine plants, PVC pipes, plastic Buddha statues, and bubbling divers. Some companies are producing artificial reef structures that look like rock piles covered in coralline algae and sprinkled with realistic-looking corals. While these setups tend to be expensive, they do provide a natural-looking reef without the demands of filtration and lighting that a real reef tank requires.

Bioload

I want to end this discussion of husbandry with a few words about the carrying capacities of saltwater tanks. In general, marine aquariums cannot hold as many fishes as equivalent-sized freshwater systems. Reasons for this include the lower capacity of salt water to hold oxygen, the increased toxicity of dissolved ammonia in the high pH of marine tanks, and the greater sensitivity of marine fishes to poor water quality.

Deciding on the carrying capacity of an aquarium is more art than science, but always start with fewer fishes than you think the tank can hold, and monitor things very carefully to make sure the system is stable. Also remember that the bigger the volume of the tank, the more stable the water quality is and the larger the holding capacity will be.

The effects of excessive bioload show up as an accumulation of pollution such as nitrates, a drop in pH, and loss of alkalinity or buffering capacity. These three problems are intimately linked, and the remedies for them are obvious: water changes and cleaning.

Pollution

Over time pollution will accumulate in your aquarium. As you add more fishes or as your fishes grow, the bioload increases, as does the amount you feed, which further increases the bioload. Much of the fish waste is readily handled by your filtration system. It does a fantastic job with the aerobic processes of converting ammonia to nitrite to nitrate but a very poor job at the anaerobic portion of converting nitrate to nitrogen, so nitrate accumulates. Nitrate is toxic, but not as acutely so as ammonia or nitrite. However, its lack of immediate toxicity leads many aquarists to ignore its cumulative effect.

It's not uncommon to have 40 to 50 ppm in a fish-only tank. I've even helped clean tanks that were consistently in the 200- to 300-ppm range, and the fish appeared fine. Scientific studies have shown, though, that exposure to high nitrate levels is detrimental to fish. I equate nitrates to smog—sure you can live in it, but it will eventually cause health issues and shorten your life. In this regard, I recommend you test monthly for nitrates and if you find the nitrates creeping up, step up your water changes.

Given the adult size of large-bodied lionfish, like this black *P. volitans*, a tank for lionfish needs plenty of open space

pH Drop

Fish metabolism and decomposition produce acids. As wastes accumulate, the amount of acid produced increases. The buffering capacity of the water is challenged by all this acid, and when it is exhausted, the pH drops, often precipitously. This severely stresses any marine fish.

Loss of Alkalinity

The naturally high alkalinity or buffering capacity (KH) of ocean water makes it resistant to changes in pH, but a heavy bioload can overwhelm the buffers, permitting an accumulation of acid and a decrease in pH. Marine salt mixes are even more heavily buffered than natural seawater, but the accumulation of acids will still eventually bring down the pH. Regular water changes provide the double benefit of removing acids and replenishing buffering capacity. This can be supplemented if whenever you add top-off water you use buffered water. This will boost alkalinity in between water changes and help avoid a potentially lethal crash in pH.

Acquiring a New Lionfish

How should you get your scorpaenid? Over the years I've frequented many local pet stores and feel most comfortable going to my old haunts where I know the owner and have seen the quality of his fish over the years. I usually prefer to shop at these places. If they have a good stock, my dollars reward them, and I build a relationship with them. It's really the best way I know to ensure getting a healthy fish. I can observe it and get the straight scoop from the owner on whether it's eating and has settled in to tank life.

Large chain pet stores are another possible source for your fish. While it's hard to build a relationship with the often-transient staff in these stores, at least you can view the fish and see whether it's eating. The Internet now provides another interesting option. The prices are usually good (though you have to figure in the cost of shipping, which is considerable), and there is a broad selection. I do shop online for fish and have been rewarded numerous times, but I've also had a few bad experiences. So *caveat emptor*—let the buyer beware. Always do online research about the establishment. Many online vendors provide a guarantee of live arrival, and some even go so far as to give a few days past arrival to ensure the fish settles in. Also understand their shipping policy. You typically have to pay for shipping again if the fish arrives dead and the dealer wants to replace it. If you're a member of a local fish society you can join with other local fish hobbyists to arrange a group purchase so the shipping costs will be defrayed among many hobbyists.

What to Look for

Impulse buys almost never work. Before buying any fish you should have suitable answers to at least these questions:

- Is the fish suitable for your expertise level of aquarium-keeping?
- Will the new fish be compatible with its tankmates?
- Does it eat?
- Do you have a quarantine tank ready for it?
- Is the new fish in excellent health?

The answer to the last question requires you to evaluate the fish's appearance and behavior. It is not hard to evaluate the first, but assessing the behavior of a sedentary fish can be more difficult. Fortunately, lionfish and their relatives are usually obviously healthy or not. A quick visual examination is all it takes to clear a fish for possible purchase. Pass on any fish that has labored breathing or is off in color or looks beat up. Include the following in your exam.

Don't Be Complacent

Remember that conditions in your aquarium will not remain the same over time. Even if you start with perfect water parameters, they will change from day to day. Both natural processes and your actions will affect them. The key to success is to follow a regimen of filtration maintenance and water changes that will regularly improve deteriorating water quality.

Head

The eyes should be bright and clear and normally set in the head. A lionfish will frequently direct its attention towards you as you peer into the tank, but a scorpionfish will not overtly look at you, and you may need to get it to move so you can see the eyes properly. Bacterial infections are often first seen as a gray cloudy film or light misty appearance in the eyes. The mouth should be intact and uninjured.

Fins

The fins should be intact and clean. Look particularly at where the fins attach to the body—any redness or scrapes? Minimally torn fins and broken fin rays are acceptable, as they will heal. A lionfish should not clamp down its fins and should respond normally by fluttering them in your presence.

Little-known gems show up occasionally in the pet store. For example, this *Sebastapistes strongia*, a relatively rare scorpionfish, would do well in a smaller tank with mellow tankmates.

Skin

The skin and scales should be uniform and well colored. Missing scales and uplifted regions are often bad signs. Many raised spots or a fuzzy appearance indicates disease. In scorpionfish look to see whether the fish has intact coverings with no major red irritated areas. In all scorpions, the cuticle may be in various states of shedding. This is okay as long as you don't observe redness or open wounds.

Body Condition

The fish should have sufficient body mass, especially through its middle and sides; a mild concave stomach is acceptable, but not one pinched inward. Make sure there is no lateral line deterioration or pitting, and no twisted curvature to the fish.

Signs of Disease

Avoid fish with open sores, spots, bumps, cloudy eyes, torn or ragged fins, or weird posturing. These signs might suggest high stress or an unhealthy fish. Keep in mind that many scorpions are uniquely colored, and white spots and raised bumps might be normal camouflage—another reason to research any species thoroughly before acquiring it.

Activity

A lionfish shouldn't be too lethargic or too hyperactive. It shouldn't be lying on the bottom or leaning, either. With other scorpaeniforms this assessment might be challenging. Using a net (not your hand!) you can stir a scorpionfish into movement. Does it swim or move normally as it tries to escape? Get the storeowner to feed the fish in front of you. A healthy lionfish will always show interest in or be aware of food.

Acclimating Your New Scorpaenids

The purpose of acclimation is simple: to adjust the water, temperature, and salinity of the shipping bag to your aquarium (or quarantine tank, ideally). Many fish are sensitive to even minor changes in parameters, so proper acclimation will ensure your new fish start their relocation successfully. I use the one-hour floating method with great success for all scorpaeniforms:

1) Turn off the tank lights.

2) Float the shipping bag in your aquarium to normalize the temperature of the shipping water to your tank for 10–15 minutes, (30 minutes for bags holding large amounts of shipping water).

3) Open the bag and roll the top edge down, creating an airspace and making the bag float upright.

4) Add about half a cup of tank water into the bag.

5) Repeat every five minutes until bag begins to sink.

6) Discard most of the water in the bag and put it back into the tank, floating.

7) Again add half a cup of tank water to the bag every five minutes.

8) Repeat until an hour has passed. Net the fish and release it into the aquarium. Discard the water in the bag. Top off the tank as necessary with new salt water. Leave the lights off for the rest of the day.

Be patient and don't rush an acclimation. Never add an airstone to the shipping water, as this may increase the pH too quickly and expose your new fish to ammonia toxicity.

If a shipped fish appears dead, go through the acclimation process anyway. Often a lifeless-looking fish is just suffering from shock and stress and revives during acclimation.

Lionfish do not normally clamp their fins together as is shown here. This specimen is likely to be unhealthy or stressed in some way.

The requirement that you research the species you intend to purchase begins even before you bring your fish home. Abnormal behavior is a major reason to pass a specimen by, but if you don't know what its normal behavior is, how can you make this judgment? For example, a *Pterois* lionfish lying on the bottom of its tank partially buried in sand is clearly a fish to avoid, while that is perfectly normal for many scorpionfish.

Nutrition

It's feeding time! These fish, which usually just lie around and spend all day in one spot, all of sudden come to life. It's only when we feed that we can witness what our scorpions do best: flashing their fins and gulping food with amazingly quick responses.

Improper nutrition is the predominant health issue for captive scorpions. In the wild, these animals eat smaller fishes and invertebrates. Unfortunately, the most common mistake new owners make is to give them live freshwater feeder fish, but you should not make that mistake.

Freshwater Feeders

Freshwater feeder fish do not provide the proper nutrition. Specifically they lack a number of marine-based fats and micronutrients. Also, in comparison to saltwater fish, many freshwater fish used as feeders contain much more fat per gram. Necroscopies of pet scorpaeniforms typically reveal hepatic lipidosis—fatty liver disease—in which the liver hypertrophies (grows excessively large), and loses ability to function properly. It is almost certain that a lionfish or scorpionfish fed exclusively with goldfish or other freshwater fish will die prematurely due to a number of feeder fish-associated problems.

Of all the freshwater live feeding choices available to the hobbyist, the feeding of ghost shrimp is the only viable one. Of course, saltwater ghost shrimp are even better if they are available. Freshwater ghost shrimp can be enriched in marine-based highly unsaturated fatty acids (HUFAs) by being fed any marine flake food or marine plant material, and I have not found a lionfish or scorpionfish yet that will refuse a ghost shrimp. I have used ghost shrimp for many years to successfully adapt difficult-to-feed scorpions (like leaf fish, seagoblins, Fu Man Chu lions, and Ambon lions) to tank life.

You should establish your new fish by temporarily using ghost shrimp for a couple of weeks to a month. After this establishment period, you should work to wean the fish off these feeders and onto marine-based prepared foods.

Weaning Your Fish

The best way to ensure a scorpion remains in proper health is to feed it a varied diet of fresh and frozen seafoods. Here are three methods I use successfully to get difficult fish to feed on non-living foods.

Fasting One of the best ways to wean a fish onto prepared foods is to withhold food for three or four days, then introduce a small intact lancefish or silverside (a saltwater fish commonly available as frozen fish food). I find it best to impale this silverside onto an acrylic or wooden rod (feeding stick) and wiggle it convincingly away from but in full view of the fish.

Fish on a String This is like the feeding stick method outlined above and can also be used after a short fast. A string loosely fastened to a silverside is used to pull the fish through the water, imitating natural swimming and initiating predator response.

Net Method This method relies on your fish familiarizing itself with food being offered in a net and is especially useful for many substrate-hugging scorpionfish. Put live ghost shrimp in a fish net and place the net in front of your new fish. As the ghost shrimp escape they are eaten by your fish. Very soon your pet will adapt to the net and equate anything coming out of the net with food. This technique works well if you use live ghost shrimp first, followed by dead but intact ghost shrimp, followed by thawed intact mysid shrimp and other foods.

It may take time to encourage your scorpion to eat non-living foods, but this weaning process is the most critical key to success. It is usually

Ghost shrimp are an excellent food for scorpaeniforms; almost all the species readily feed on them.

easier to get a younger fish to switch over to non-living foods than an older animal. In my experience a hungry lionfish is a brave lionfish, and the use of starvation prior to offering prepared foods is often a key to success. But you can certainly mix portions of all three techniques. If feeding live foods is desired, grass shrimp (harvested from salt water), fiddler crabs, small shrimp, and saltwater "minnows" are good choices.

Feeding Schedule

After being weaned onto prepared foods, scorpions often learn to beg for food. Don't give in. Lionfish and their kin are gluttonous and, if fed continuously, will grow too quickly (possibly resulting in health issues and a shortened life span) and generate undesirable amounts of waste in the tank water. It is important not to offer large prey items or large chunks of food, as such are implicated in scorpaeniform deaths.

According to Michaels (Michaels, 1998), lionfish will occasionally kill themselves by overeating. While I have not experienced this, I have found that lionfish will eat to the point of regurgitation, and this indicates severe overeating. Offer multiple smaller food items rather than one large one. In fact, if a lionfish is given the choice between a large fish and many small ones, it will normally choose to eat the smaller fish first. In the wild, a lionfish will consume from 1 to 11 small to medium-sized prey items per feeding, then retire to a hiding spot to digest the food for a day or so, later repeating this process.

I recommend feeding adult lionfish to the point of seeing a small bulge in their abdomen two to three times weekly; juvenile and young lions can be fed four to five times weekly. Note that this means there will be regular fast days for your fish. This feeding/fasting cycle replicates the normal feeding schedule in the wild, and will extend the life span of these sedentary predators.

What to Feed

You should rotate your scorpion's diet through as many marine foods as you can find at your local grocery store. Yes, that's right—human food. I make a once-monthly trip to the local food mart to purchase uncooked Gulf shrimp (with their shells on), prawn, lobster tail, crab meat, strips/chunks of whatever marine fish is on sale, squid, octopus, mussels. To these I add silversides or lancefish.

Preparing Foods and Supplements When I get all this food home, I process it all into chunks. I rinse the meats with water but leave the shells on the prawn/shrimp and don't do much more than cut them into small bite-sized pieces. Next I mix all the chunks in

Net feeding is one method to ensure that sedentary scorpionfish, leaf fish, and similar species are getting enough food.

a bowl, add a few drops of a marine highly unsaturated fatty acid (HUFA) booster and also a liquid or powdered fish vitamin product. I have also heard that adding garlic juice or a small piece of garlic stimulates both a feeding response and potentially aids a fish's immune system, so you might want to add this as well. I do not recommend you feed cooked, steamed, blanched, or otherwise processed foods to your fish, as cooking can reduce many nutrients.

I place portions equal to one feeding's worth into plastic sandwich bags, flatten the bags, seal them, and stack them into my freezer. I try to incorporate at least four different fresh seafoods in each feeding. To feed I take out one baggie of food, thaw it at room temperature (or place it in the microwave for a few seconds to defrost but not cook), open the baggie, and add the food slowly into the water current.

A scorpion may go off its feed for no apparent reasons, and a fish that refuses to feed can make its owner very nervous, especially considering the fish has been a champ when it came to eating before. Similar to the psychological anorexia in humans, acute fish anorexia—in which an animal suddenly stops eating and refuses to feed—is usually caused by a major stress such as disease, tankmate aggression, or capture and transport stressors, and once you identify and resolve the issues, the fish should begin to feed again.

Many lionfish owners will experience another type of anorexia. Sometimes a long-term captive fish that has eaten for months to years all of a sudden stops eating; it appears somewhat interested in food, but never eats. Such chronic anorexia is a complex problem, frequently difficult to solve, and in my experience results from the accumulation of long-term nutritional issues.

One of the common food items strongly associated with chronic anorexia is freeze-dried krill. I'm not exactly sure why, but many hobbyists have reported that their long-term captive lionfish have developed anorexia after months and months of being fed krill-based diets. That said, instead of trying to solve the riddle of why the fish isn't eating, it's best to take action and attempt to get the fish back to eating again. A healthy lionfish can go for weeks without food, but you want to solve the problem before it's too late. Here are three things you can do. Try them in the order listed and move on to the next if necessary.

Live Foods Nothing stimulates the feeding response better than a wiggling, swimming fish or shrimp. Add live fish or ghost shrimp and see whether the fish will eat. In a fish that has been fed months of prepared foods this is frequently sufficient.

Freshwater Dip Freshwater dips are used to remove external parasites and frequently have a side effect of causing the fish to defecate. Since we want to ensure the non-feeding fish is not impacted, a freshwater dip using temperature-adjusted and buffered water for no more than ten minutes (four to six minutes for juveniles) can work in our favor. You can repeat this dip after 36 hours if necessary. As soon as the fish defecates you can remove it.

Tube Feeding Tube-feeding is the most invasive method, but it may be necessary to give your fish enough energy to keep going while you figure out a permanent solution. Because of the delicate nature

The Hand That Feeds

Although some scorpaeniforms may be difficult to wean off live foods, the most common aquarium specimens— the pteroines and the scorpaenines— usually learn quickly that the funny-looking bipeds bring food. Once a fish learns this, it will snap up anything that is dropped into its tank.

of this operation and the extreme potential for envenomation when handling a scorpionfish this closely, you will need to enlist a trained professional. The process utilizes a syringe and a flexible tube to place liquefied food (a fish or shrimp slurry) directly into the animal's stomach. The amount of food administered should equal 3 percent of the animal's body weight, or just enough food to cause a slight distension of its belly. In most cases, the use of an anesthetic is required to sedate the fish so the tube can be inserted safely. Once the fish has been fed, the tube is gently withdrawn and the fish is moved to a quarantine and recovery tank.

Scorpaeniforms will eat a lot of the same seafood that humans do, so you can purchase a large percentage of your fish's food at the grocery store.

Diseases & Disorders

The good news is that scorpaeniform fish are pretty resistant to disease. They can get sick, but they do so well after the canary-in-the-coal-mine fish have already succumbed.

Identifying Illness

It's fairly easy to spot a fish in distress. Common signs include:

- Abnormal swimming is usually one of the first symptoms of something being wrong with your lionfish. This is not so obvious with a ground-crawling scorpionfish. When you watch the fish, its swimming motion can appear drunk; the fish will swim in circles or simply drift with the current. Frequently the drunken swimming is mixed in with sinking to the bottom or the fish's being unable to raise itself, or its floating aimlessly, incapable of holding its position in the water column. Severe health problems can even make a fish swim upside down with its belly pointing towards the surface.

Difficult-to-feed scorpionfish can be placed in a "weaning basket", a suspended container placed in the main tank. Utilizing the basket, you can keep a watchful eye on the feeding of a new fish.

- Increased respiration or labored breathing is an important warning sign. If you notice your fish is rapidly moving its gill covers in and out, or what appears like gasping, this indicates something has gone awry, and you should immediately increase aeration and carry out a series of water changes. Various scorpionfish have different respiratory rates, and it is therefore difficult to say how fast a healthy fish should breathe. However, if you observe your fish while it's healthy, you'll be able to notice if it starts to struggle for oxygen.
- A sickly fish that does not feel good will often dampen its colors. Loss of coloration can be brought on by virtually anything, from skin problems and internal disease to low levels of oxygen.
- If a fish refuses food for extended periods, it is likely ill.
- Visible cysts, sores, and lesions indicate that a fish needs help.
- ADR (ain't doin right) is a phrase used by veterinarians to describe an animal that just isn't acting normal. Obviously, normal is different for every species, and since each fish is an individual, it will be up to you as the owner and observer to notice when your fish is ADR.

Feeding Cautions

While it is very convenient that most lionfish and scorpionfish easily associate their keepers with food, there are two inherent problems with this behavior. One is that these appealing fish also quickly learn to beg, and it is very important to resist and not to overfeed them. The other is that the fish thereby lose fear and inhibition, so they are quite likely to approach you when you—your hand and arm—enter the aquarium. This makes accidental envenomation much more likely.

Parasites and Pathogens

These diseases are listed in order of the frequency in which I've experienced them.

Marine Ich (*Cryptocaryon irritans* or White Spot Disease) Marine ich is the most common disease problem in a marine aquarium. Most hobbyists recognize the white spots, similar to sprinkled salt, on an affected fish. Unfortunately this visual clue is also the reason for difficulty in eradicating the parasite—by the time you recognize it, the infection is well under way. Healthy scorpaenids are pretty resistant to ich, as they're covered with a layer of dermis called the cuticle that is fairly tough for the protozoan that causes the disease to penetrate. A stressed or sickly scorpaenid is much more susceptible to infection.

Cryptocaryon irritans, the disease's causative organism, is a ciliated protozoan with a four-stage life cycle lasting approximately 30 days in which adults (called trophonts) attach to and bore underneath the scales of the fish, ingesting the fish's fluids (days one to seven). They then drop off into the water column and attach to rockwork and substrate (18 hours later). Next they encapsulate into a tomont stage, divide into hundreds of new daughter cells (days 8 to 28), and hatch into thousands of immature freeswimming theronts that must find a host within about 24 hours or they will perish.

Since these parasites are generally susceptible to medications only during the freeswimming stage, and since the disease can persist in a barren aquarium for a month without fish hosts, it is a difficult thing to eradicate. And, since scorpaeniforms are reported to be sensitive to most chemicals used to treat ich, it is obviously much better to avoid getting the disease into your system. That's where a quarantine regimen comes into play. (See below.)

Bacterial Infections

Bacterial infections generally occur when a fish's immune system is suppressed by stress or trauma. Since pathogenic bacteria are always present in aquarium water, they are always ready to take advantage of a fish with a weakened immune system.

Careful observation of your fish is the first line of defense against illness. You should know your fish well enough to see subtle changes of behavior or appearance that could indicate a problem.

The most common bacterial disease I have seen on lionfish is fin rot, a bacterial infection in which the fins, or where the fins attach to the body of the lionfish, bear reddish inflamed regions or visible body ulcers, then within days start to decay or melt away. The only treatment for this issue is to isolate the sick fish and treat with antibiotics in a hospital tank. I've had good success with an extended bath of nitrofurazone (250 mg per 10 gallons of water).

Cloudy eyes indicate a bacterial infection in which the eyes of the fish appear to have a hazy white cloud on them. It is most easily seen when the fish is turned a bit sideways to allow the light to reflect off the eye. Cloudy eyes are usually a secondary bacterial infection brought on by stress. The key is two-fold: one, eliminate the stressor, and two, resolve the bacterial infection. Cloudy eyes frequently appear on new fish and fish that are being harassed or living in declining water conditions. The first plan of action is to do a few water changes over a three- to five-day period. If the eyes don't clear up, isolate the fish in a hospital tank and use an approved antibiotic per the manufacturer's instructions.

Injury Injuries arising from encounters with tankmates are a common problem with scorpaeniforms. Many fish love to peck at the flowing fins of a lionfish or worse, they think the raised camouflaged skin tags on a scorpionfish are edible sponges. This can result in serious cuts, deep-tissue bruises, and lacerations.

Whatever the injury, the treatment is universal. Remove the offending fish from the tank, place the wounded scorpion in the hospital tank with new clean water, and simply monitor your fish for any signs of infection. If the wounds heal completely, return the fish to the display tank. If the wounds become infected, treat with an appropriate antibacterial medicine per the manufacturer's instructions.

Viral Infections Viral diseases are rare in saltwater fish, but there is one viral infection that I've seen numerous times on lionfish fins: lymphocystis. This is a herpes virus, and it affects connective tissue and creates whitish warts on the edges of a fish's fins and around the mouth. Any fish exhibiting symptoms of lymphocystis should be removed and placed in a quarantine tank. This disease is rarely fatal, but it can be disfiguring, and currently there is no medication for it. The good news is once your new fish settles in and feels at ease, the fish's immune system will clear this viral infection, usually in a few weeks.

External Parasites There are a whole host of external parasites that affect saltwater fish; the good news is that many of them don't cause many problems in scorpions, and external parasites are easy to recognize and fairly easy to eliminate. A lionfish

It can be difficult to see external injuries and infections in scorpionfish (*Scorpaenopsis macrochir* shown here) because their coloration and skin projections are so complicated.

suffering from an external parasite will frequently go off its feed, appear listless, and scratch (called flashing) against rockwork and decorations. The most obvious sign of an external parasite is that you can see it: tiny dark or white spots, worm-like creatures, or amphipods. Frequently you'll find the greatest density near the head and gills, as these regions have the greatest blood flow.

Once you've confirmed an external parasite the easiest treatment is a freshwater dip. (See the anorexia section for the protocol.) Severe infections may require multiple dips 36 hours apart followed by quarantine and medication. Follow the manufacturer's recommendations for concentrations and treatment times. After treatment leave the fish in the hospital/quarantine tank for at least three weeks to ensure the parasites are all eliminated.

Excessive Cuticle Shedding

Although not a disease in itself, excessive cuticle shedding can be used as an indicator of poor health. A sick scorpion will often shed far more than normal, and this is usually a symptom of a larger problem such as high stress, poor water quality, or parasites. The solution to excessive cuticle shedding is to search for the offending problem. Remove any harassing tankmates to reduce stress, do multiple water changes, clean your filters, dim the lighting, and observe your fish for any signs of disease. A common cause of excessive cuticle shedding is deteriorating water quality, so that's a good place to start searching.

Lockjaw

Lockjaw or jaw dislocation occurs when the fish's mouthparts stay fixed in the open position. I have observed this on many occasions. It is unclear what causes this problem,

A Word About Medications

Use medications only as a last resort after you've exhausted all other means. Make sure you have perfect water quality and no harassing tankmates. Seek out the source of the problem and do what you can to resolve it.

Only then should you decide to medicate. When you must medicate your fish, do so in a hospital tank and follow the manufacturer's instruction to the letter—many drugs are toxic at higher concentrations and ineffective at lower concentrations. Always complete the full cycle of treatment.

but I have observed fish unintentionally ingesting substrate during feeding or banging their mouthparts into rockwork when hunting food items, and this may account for at least part of the problem. Over the course of a few days fish with this condition typically are able to work their jaws closed again, but the alignment of the jaw is usually not perfect, and their jaws frequently dislocate again.

Quarantine and Hospital Tanks

Quarantine everything. I can't emphasize this point enough. Quarantine, or else the first time you introduce a new fish that brings an illness into your aquarium, you'll be kicking yourself—especially if the new bug wipes out one or more of your prized specimens!

Quarantine Tank

A quarantine tank is a stand-alone supplemental tank used to temporarily house fish before they are added to your collection. Set up similar to your display tank, a quarantine tank can incorporate filtration, heaters, minimal decorations, and lighting to maintain similar conditions to your display tank.

Normally the fish kept in a quarantine tank are your newly acquired specimens, but you can also use a quarantine tank to hold any fish of interest and keep it under observation. A quarantine tank allows you to carefully observe any physical and behavioral issues, as well as ensure the new fish is eating properly. During the time of quarantine you should perform daily observation and examination to gather insight into whether this new fish will successfully compete in your display tank. Importantly, the quarantine tank's role is to minimize stress and allow the new fish to acclimate to your tank conditions. A good quarantine tank for mid-bodied or small scorpions is 20 gallons (75 liters), while a 30-gallon (115-liter) tank can be used for large-bodied lionfish. Quarantine tanks should contain at a minimum an established filter system (hang-on-back or established sponge filter), a few PVC tubes or rings for hiding spots, a heater, minimal to no substrate, and dim lighting. A minimum quarantine period of at least three to four weeks is recommended for new arrivals.

Be a Pioneer

The greatest hurdle to raising captive-spawned scorpaeniform fry is one shared with most popular reef fishes: the fish hatch as planktonic larvae. These float helplessly in the ocean currents with countless other very small algae and animals. The tiny fry eat even tinier creatures, and many prey only on very specific plankton. The key to successful captive breeding is usually discovering and providing a reliable food source that the fry will eat and that will provide them appropriate nutrition. We have not yet reached that point for scorpions. Perhaps you will be the first one to succeed with a scorpaeniform species!

Hospital Tank

Your quarantine tank can double as a hospital tank. Of course, if you have to treat a fish during quarantine, it will be in the quarantine tank, but if a fish in your display tank becomes ill, you should move it to a separate tank before treating it.

Never add medication to your main tank. Many medications have potent antibiotic effects and will kill off your biofiltration. They can also harm or kill non-target animals, and not only sessile or ornamental invertebrates in a reef-type system, but also other fish. As mentioned above, scorpions can be sensitive to medications. It's bad enough if therapy kills the diseased animal, but you don't want to risk fish that aren't even sick! Additionally, by using a hospital tank with a much smaller volume than your display tank, you'll require less medication and make it much easier to control and monitor dosages. Finally, substrates and rocks (such as crushed coral and live rock and even the aquarium glass) can take up medications. This not only renders the treatment much less effective, it permanently restricts the use of these materials in the future—many years later the chemicals in them can kill invertebrates placed in with them. All of this also underscores the importance of quarantine. If an unquarantined fish introduces disease into your display tank, you are in trouble.

Lionfish and Scorpionfish Reproduction

Ornamental scorpaeniforms have not yet been successfully bred in captivity. We can get the fish to spawn, but the resulting fry have been impossible to raise. This section presents a few details about what we do know in regard to scorpion reproduction. Hopefully aquarists like you will continue to move the understanding and breeding of these fantastic fishes forward.

The reproductive modes of the Scorpaeniformes are extremely varied and range from

The furnishings in a quarantine tank should be kept to a minimum and a substrate is not strictly necessary. *Scorpaena brasiliensis* is shown here.

oviparity (egg laying) to viviparity (embryo developing inside the female) and even zygoparity or embryoparity (spawning of internally fertilized eggs or embryos) (Koya, 2007). Scorpaeniforms can be divided into two distinct subtypes based on the structure of their ovaries: cystovarian type II-1 and cystovarian type II-3. These ovary structures are not found in any other teleost fishes and are considered a primitive feature. Of interest to us hobbyists are species that possess cystovarian type II-3 and have a common feature of spawning: a floating egg mass encompassed by gelatinous material (Fishelson, 1975).

A Beginning

Two lionfishes have been observed spawning in the wild and in captivity, the dwarf fuzzy lionfish, *Dendrochirus brachypterus,* and the volitans lionfish, *Pterois volitans.* It is not known whether all other scorpaenids follow the same spawning behaviors. Dwarf fuzzy lionfish are really the only lionfish in which sexual determination can be made easily, but keeping groups of three or more of the same species will increase your chance of getting male/female pairs—the obvious first requirement for successful spawning.

Most species of lionfish are impossible to sex, but in *D. barberi* males (left) have larger, broader heads and longer pectoral fins than the females (right). Males also have six or more dark stripes on these fins while females have four to six. These sexual differences are true for *D. brachypterus* as well.

A courting male dwarf fuzzy lion will form a harem group of several females. During this time, the male will become aggressive, darken, then intensify in coloration. His pectoral and body stripes become less visible, whereas gravid females take on a lighter hue, with many areas of the body becoming light.

Spawning begins as the male swims over to a female and nudges her, sometimes pressing her side. After circling the female several times, the male rises to the surface pursued by the eager female. During this spawning ascension, the pair will corkscrew upward, and at the peak of their ascension the female will flutter her pectoral fins. This rising and sinking process is repeated several times until finally the female releases an egg mass that is quickly fertilized. The gelatinous egg mass then floats at the surface for 24 hours before it starts to decompose. Depending on species, the egg mass can contain from 1000 to 15,000 eggs.

Other spawning observations include a photographic record of *P. radiata* in the wild during their spawning ascensions and release of the egg mass. These behaviors were identical to what I described for the dwarf fuzzy lionfish. A hobbyist report of *P. russelli* spawning in a 300-gallon display aquarium was also quite similar to that of *D. brachypterus*, and the spawn resulted in a gelatinous egg mass. These reports suggest that *Pterois* and *Dendrochirus* have similar breeding behaviors. I have had breeding activity occur on two occasions and with two separate pairs of waspfish and Ambon lionfish; while there was no spawning ascension, the end result was a small egg ball.

Eggs, Then What?

It is thought that the gelatinous egg mass mimics a bad-tasting comb jellyfish, and one hobbyist reported that an egg mass settled on an algae covered rock in his tank and quickly killed off the algae, suggesting the egg mass itself might be toxic. The lionfish embryo's head and eyes become apparent after 18 hours. The gelatinous mass decomposes within 24 hours due to bacterial action, releasing the developing eggs. The fry hatch 36 hours later as poorly developed prolarvae lacking eye pigment, a digestive tract and functional fins, and are approximately 1.0-to-1.25 mm in *D. brachypterus*, and 1.52-to-1.58 mm for *P. lunulata*, attached to a yolk sac. The fry consume the yolk over the next four to six days, at which point the fry will feed immediately on available plankton. There is one report that the larvae feed on ciliates, and others have tried field-collected plankton. The larvae settle out of the plankton after a period of approximately 25 to 40 days, at a size of 10–12 mm in length. So far no attempts have been successful at keeping the fry alive longer than 10 to 13 days.

The major hurdle in developing protocols for raising marine ornamental fry is typically finding a suitable food for the planktonic stage. The best advice I can offer about feeding the lionfish fry is that we consider adapting the techniques developed by hobbyists attempting to raise another difficult fish with incredibly small larvae—pygmy angelfish, *Centropyge* spp. For example, they often use a kreisel (circular-current) tank to ensure the delicate fry remain in suspension and use copepod nauplii as the first food. Hopefully we will soon discover the keys to raising lionfish and scorpionfish in our aquariums.

Egg mass of the dwarf fuzzy lionfish (*D. brachypterus*) produced in a hobbyist's tank. Unfortunately, no one has yet succeeded in rearing baby scorpaeniforms in captivity.

Species Guide: The Lions

Lionfish are members of the subfamily Pteroinae within the family Scorpaenidae, with five genera and about sixteen species. Two of the genera and at least eleven of the lionfish species make their way regularly into the aquarium hobby. The species most often seen in the home aquarium are in the genera *Pterois* and *Dendrochirus*. *Dendrochirus* species are often referred to as dwarf lionfishes and have the upper rays of the pectoral fin branched and connected by a membrane. In *Pterois* the upper pectoral rays are free from the webbing membrane.

While lionfish generally do not eat corals or other sessile invertebrates, they will consume many motile species, including cleaner shrimp.

Lionfishes range in size anywhere from 4 inches (10 cm) to about 17 inches (43 cm). Most species have a very wide distribution throughout the western Pacific Ocean, but a few have a restricted range. The Hawai`ian lionfish *P. sphex* is endemic to the waters surrounding the islands of Hawai`i, and the Japanese luna lionfish, *P. lunulata,* is only found only in the cold waters off Japan.

The Lion Tank

The general description in the previous chapter suits a tank for lionfish. The specific aquascaping should be varied to best fit the species you will be housing.

Aquascaping

Many of the dwarf lionfishes spend much of their day hiding or resting upside down in caves and therefore require rockwork and cave structures to make them feel comfortable. The Fu Man Chu Lionfish, *D. biocellatus,* will traverse through your rockwork, hiding almost exclusively until dinnertime. On the other hand, *Pterois* species will spend their day out in the open, resting along the rockwork tops or hanging in a corner, and therefore a more open tank structure would work nicely. For those interested in keeping a lions' den setup with multiple lionfish and a few scorpionfish, a good mixture of caves and rock nooks combined with open spaces will allow all the species to find their happy place. Lionfish are not known to be particularly territorial and will share their cave or other place of refuge with members of their own species or other lionfish species. Again remember that a lionfish is only interested in another fish if it can fit into its mouth. I have never experienced a lionfish harassing or tormenting a tankmate that was not considered food.

Reefs?

Lionfish can be kept in a reef tank, but be aware that while they have no interest in sessile invertebrates like corals, they will eat any small fish or ornamental shrimp that can fit into their mouths, including cleaner shrimp. Note also that these heavy-bodied, heavy-feeding fish present a much larger bioload than most reefkeepers allow.

Lionfish usually won't attack starfish, such as the chocolate chip star, and these animals are useful for cleaning the tank.

Clean-up Crews

I like adding cleanup crews to lionfish and scorpionfish tanks. Cleanup crews are essentially detritus-feeding invertebrates whose function is to scavenge remnants of food, detritus, and algae. They perform a valuable— essential, even—function in the home aquarium, and many of them are quite interesting to observe feeding. Most lionfish ignore starfish (Asteroidea), sea cucumbers (Holothuroidea), sea urchins (Echinoidea), cerith snails (*Cerithium*), and hermit crabs (*Paguristes, Pagurus*). In a lions' den type of tank

The red eye of the green lionfish sets it apart from similar species. This one was photographed in the Hawai`ian Islands.

setup, a few larger hermit crabs (slightly smaller than a golf ball in size) scavenge the substrate much better than you can with a vacuum. I'm a big fan of keeping starfish in scorpionfish tanks, as they add movement (albeit slowly) and many of the colored starfish (like *Protoreaster linckii, Pentaceraster* sp., and the chocolate chip starfish, *Protoreaster nodosus*) are absolutely gorgeous. Just make sure that these starfish get a chunk of food every once in a while; the rest of the time they will cruise the tank in search of food remnants.

Tankmates

While lionfish ignore any tankmate too large to eat (generally about half the size of the lionfish or bigger, but be careful!), the reverse is not always true. I've had success with tangs, large wrasses such as the harlequin wrasse, *Bodianus eclancheri*, planktonic-feeding triggers (*Xanthichthys*), Niger triggers (*Odonus*), and other scorpions. Many triggerfish, especially the *Balistoides, Pseudobalistes, Balistes,* and *Rhinecanthus* triggers, make very poor tankmates for lionfishes. Often clown triggers will attack and break off the venomous spines of a lionfish. Puffers will also pluck the long flowing pectoral fins of lionfishes. I personally experienced an emperor angelfish, *Pomacanthus imperator,* that decided to evoke fear in my lionfish by picking on their fins and generally harassing everyone. That fish was promptly removed.

If you want to keep more than one lionfish, just keep in mind two rules: one, larger lionfish will eat smaller lionfish, and two, male lionfish of the same species will fight, sometimes seriously.

Dwarf Lionfishes

Four of the five *Dendrochirus* species and one *Pterois* species are usually considered as dwarf lions because of their smaller size and more sedentary, bottom-dwelling habits. It is thought that all *Dendrochirus* lions form harems.

Dendrochirus barberi

Common Names: Green lionfish, Hawai`ian lionfish.
Size: 6 inches (15 cm)
Distribution: East-central Pacific—Hawai`i and the Johnston Atoll.

This species looks like a dwarf fuzzy lion except for its duller coloration and bright red eyeball (dwarf fuzzy lions have an iridescent blue-green eye). It is found in lagoons and clear-reef areas at depths to 50 meters (160 feet). It is typically hidden during the day in holes and crevices. A few dive reports have suggested these lions sit at the base of coral heads while awaiting passing fish and invertebrates. The species is thought to feed primarily on crustaceans.

D. barberi is rarely encountered in the hobby, probably because it is brown/gray/green and considered less attractive than dwarf fuzzy lions. The key identifying feature of this fish is the solid red eyeball. Green lionfish have the same requirements and care as the very common dwarf fuzzy lion. They are a hardy aquarium fish and will readily adapt to tank life provided you give them

A Lionfish by Any Other Name

As with almost all aquarium fishes, common names for lionfish are completely unreliable in identifying species. Scientific names cannot be trusted, either, since exporters, importers, and dealers will often slap on a scientific name based on their best guess (after all, they don't come out of the sea with name tags!). It takes some experience to learn to recognize the various species, and in some cases even experienced aquarists cannot make a positive identification of a lionfish in a dealer's tank. So what should you do?

Easy: learn to identify lionfish to the genus level. Almost all the specimens you find for sale will be either *Dendrochirus* or *Pterois*. Knowing which you are dealing with will tell you roughly what size the mature fish will be, which answers most husbandry questions.

plenty of hiding spots and caves. You will probably have to establish a green lionfish by using live ghost shrimp and a weaning it over to prepared foods. Larger specimens have been observed fighting with other similar-looking lionfish.

Dendrochirus biocellatus

Common Names: Double-ocellated scorpionfish, Fu Man Chu lionfish, ocellated lionfish, twinspot lionfish, two-eyed lionfish, two-spot turkeyfish.
Size: Maximum 5 inches (13 cm)
Distribution: Widespread throughout the tropics from the Indian Ocean to the western Pacific.

With its bright orange and black colorations, the two eyespots on the rear dorsal fin area, and two whisker-like appendages extending from the lower jaw, the Fu Man Chu lionfish is unmistakable. This is also the most diminutive lionfish. It is found at depths to 40 meters (130 feet), usually on reef faces and reef slopes. This is a secretive fish,

Fu Man Chu lions are small, shy lionfish that tend to do poorly in captivity. They are difficult to wean off live food.

found primarily as a solitary individual hanging upside down in darkened caves or crevices by day. At night the Fu Man Chu makes its way through reef rubble to feed, rarely exposing itself to the open. During feeding the Fu Man Chu lion will shake its head from side to side as it approaches its prey, and the eyespots on its dorsal fin will darken and lighten. Fu Man Chu lionfish act more like scorpionfish than lionfish in that they tend to crawl or hop on pelvic fins across the substrate instead of swimming. When confronted, they prefer to not give up their position until the last minute.

This species can be readily identified by two elongated feeler-like tentacles (whiskers) that protrude from either side of the mouth, giving the fish the distinctive Fu Man Chu mustache. Additionally, two ocelli (eye-spots) appear on the second dorsal fin. The fish is red-orange with blackish specks and banding. The two solid pectoral fins resemble fans from a Spanish dancer; they are circular, with the lower fin rays forming angular points. This fish is a poor swimmer; instead, it tends to scurry across the substrate and will occasionally hop.

The prey-stalking behavior of *D. biocellatus* is remarkable. Once a prey item has been identified, the fish will approach and begin to shake its head and gill covers from side to side. When in range of the food item, the lionfish will begin to rhythmically twitch its dorsal spines back and forth, and as it readies to gulp the prey item it vibrates the lower portions of its pectoral fins.

This is one of the more difficult lionfishes to keep in the home aquarium. They ship very poorly and they don't readily wean from live to prepared foods. The species is among the most shy and cautious of the lionfishes I have ever owned, and it is imperative that caves and hiding spots are made available for it to hide. Initially, individuals spend much of their time hiding in the rockwork and will come out only to feed. These fish will have problems competing with fast-swimming fish for food, and unless they are target fed, will starve. Live ghost shrimp should be among the first foods offered to establish this dwarf lion on an aquarium diet; once it is comfortable and begins coming out from hiding, the aquarist can begin to wean the fish onto prepared foods. I have had great success using frozen *Mysis* shrimp as an enticing prepared food by simply thawing the frozen *Mysis* and squirting them out of a tube in front of the hungry Fu Man Chu. Over the years, I have kept three Fu Man Chu lionfish, and it took many months to wean the slowest one from live foods.

Out of all the lionfish I have kept, the Fu Man Chu is one of the more aggressive towards same-species fish. I have not been able to introduce two Fu Man Chu lions into my 180-gallon tank without having one harassing the other to the point of sickness.

If you keep two Fu Man Chu lions in the same aquarium they will initially avoid each other, followed by the dominant fish's stalking and harassing the newly introduced one. The only time I've not witnessed this harassment was when introducing what must have been a fish of the opposite sex. Although reports suggest that all male *Dendrochirus* lions form harems, I have only observed pair formation in the home aquarium.

Dendrochirus brachypterus

Common Names: Dwarf lionfish, dwarf fuzzy lion, featherfish, short-spined butterfly cod, short-spined scorpionfish, shortfin firefish, shortfin lionfish, shortfin turkeyfish, shortspined butterfly cod, zebra firefish.

Size: 7½ inches (17 cm)

Distribution: Indo-West Pacific, from East Africa and the Red Sea to southern Japan, Australia, and Micronesia.

This is a heavy-bodied dwarf, often appearing with a color scheme containing a good deal of brown, gray, red, and yellow, mixed with red markings. Dwarf fuzzy lions are aptly named in reference to their fuzzy scale appearance. They have very large pectoral fins, with almost no emerging ray tips. This is one of the most personable marine fishes, quickly recognizing its owner and responding excitedly to the one who brings food.

These lionfish are found on reef flats, in shallow lagoons, and along coast reefs up to 30 meters (100 feet) deep. During the day the fish are found hanging upside down underneath rock ledges and overhangs or found resting among rubble and soft corals. At dawn and dusk they become very active and swim about in search of food. They feed on crabs, shrimp, and polychaete worms. Rather than capturing one large food item, this lion will consume a number of smaller items.

In the wild, dwarf fuzzy lions are found singly or in small

The dwarf fuzzy lionfish is probably the most suitable dwarf lion for the home aquarium. They are hardy and quickly adapt to prepared foods.

groups. Small harems composed of one dominant male, up to several females, and a subordinate male have been reported. *D. brachypterus* is the only obviously sexually dimorphic lionfish species, and it spawns frequently in the home aquarium.

This is probably the best of the dwarf lions for an aquarium—hardy, disease resistant, readily weaned onto prepared foods, and actively swimming. These fish have a unique fuzzy texture to their scales and possess semicircular pectoral fins that are decorated with stripes and patterns. The fin rays are short and connected with solid webbing.

These lionfish should be kept in the aquarium with plenty of hiding spots. They are not very difficult to wean onto prepared foods. All of my dwarf fuzzy lionfish learned quickly to swim towards me whenever I walk into the room, and they continue to swim and beg for food as long as I'm present.

This species comes in three color varieties: drab brownish, beautiful reddish, and a rare yellow form. Of course, combinations of reds and yellows and browns and reds exist as well. The most common in fish stores are mixtures, but I have seen a few solid red specimens, and I've come across two solid yellow ones in the past ten years.

Adult male dwarf fuzzy lions are readily identified by having a larger head, longer pectoral fins (the fin tips reach past the caudal peduncle), and six to ten bands (or stripes) on their pectoral fins. Females have only four to six stripes. In the wild, they live singly or in groups of three to ten individuals, and in a home aquarium of 100 gallons (400 liters) or greater it is possible to keep a large dominant male and several females. I have kept a breeding trio for many years, but in smaller tanks only one specimen is recommended, as dwarf fuzzy lions will harass conspecifics when crowded together.

Dendrochirus zebra

Common Names: Butterfly scorpionfish, dwarf lionfish, dwarf zebra lionfish, fan dancer, many-spotted butterfly cod, zebra butterfly cod, zebra firefish, zebra lionfish, zebra turkeyfish.

Zebra lionfish resting on coral in the waters off Sipidan, an island to the northeast of Borneo. This species is common in the aquarium trade.

Size: Maximum 10 inches (25 cm)

Distribution: Indo-West Pacific, from the Red Sea and East Africa to southern Japan and Australia

Among the more common lionfishes in the hobby, these dwarf zebras have beautiful webbed pectoral fins and are readily identified by the presence of two white spots on the caudal peduncle and by a dark spot on the lower portion of the operculum and concentric bands on the inner portion of the pectoral fins. The pectoral fin membranes extend almost all the way to the fin ray tips and form a solid web. The body pattern consists of alternating dark brown and light brown stripes.

Although they can reach larger sizes, most specimens are 6–8 inches (15–20 cm). They are found in lagoons, reef flats, and fore-reef slopes up to 35 meters (115 feet) deep. They spend the day hidden among the coral rubble, rockwork, and coral boulders. Dive reports suggest that they will also hide among sponges and sea fans awaiting passing food. This fish prefers sheltered water conditions and limited current. Stomach content analysis reveals that it feeds mainly on crabs and shrimp, but occasionally on small fish. It eats small prey—up to ten items per night. Although this is a crepuscular species, males have been observed locating female fish during daylight hours.

According to Michaels (Michaels, 1998), dwarf zebra lionfish establish territories. When two females meet they do not fight, but two males tend to fight when they cross paths. A male's territory may include several females, and these females aggregate at a rendezvous site when gravid.

Husbandry of this lion is exactly the same as for *D. brachypterus*. These fish may behave aggressively towards any species of *Dendrochirus*, so it is recommended to house them in a larger tank if you plan on keeping more than one; provide plenty of rock caves and hiding spaces. This species demonstrates very subtle sexual differences, and I have never been able to sex individuals by appearance. Males are said to have slightly larger bodies than females, and supposedly their heads are more robust. Just before spawning females will change color by taking on a brilliant white coloration while becoming darker through the midsection

Pterois sphex

Common Names: Hawai`ian lionfish, Hawai`ian turkeyfish, sphex lionfish.
Size: 8½ inches (22 cm)
Distribution: Endemic to Hawai`i.

The other endemic Hawai`ian lion, this fish looks like a miniature *P. antennata* lion, as the pectoral fins are extremely similar, but the sphex lion's fins are shorter, less colorful, and more clubbed in appearance. It lives at depths up to 120 meters (390 feet) in lagoons and on reef slopes. During the day *P. sphex* hides under rock ledges and in caves, coming out at dusk to feed on crustaceans.

This is an excellent

Hawai`ian lionfish are rare in the hobby, but they tend to do well when kept in the same conditions as antennata lions, a species with which the Hawai`ian is often confused.

hardy lionfish for the home aquarium, but it doesn't usually make its way into trade. It is seldom collected and therefore seldom available, and it tends to be much more expensive than similarly shipped lionfishes. When it does come into the trade it is frequently misidentified as *P. antennata*, even though its pectoral fins clearly look different. So stumbling upon a sphex lionfish is much like finding a two-headed penny: lucky. If you can get one, it will do very well in the home aquarium.

Husbandry for this lionfish is exactly the same as caring for *P. antennata*, covered next. Individuals often act aggressively toward other similar-sized lionfish, especially if kept in smaller tanks.

Midsized Lionfishes

As noted above, "dwarf" lionfish are generally smaller but also more sedentary, a bit closer in behavior to their scorpionfish cousins. Our arbitrary divisions here reflect their habits and their care in the aquarium rather than biological categories. So while the "midsized" lions do tend to be larger, they also stay up in the water column like the largest species.

Pterois antennata

Common Names: Antennata lion, banded lionfish, broadbarred firefish, ragged-finned firefish, ragged-finned scorpionfish, rough-scaled firefish, scorpion miles, spotfin lionfish.
Size: 8–9 inches (20–23 cm)
Distribution: Throughout the Indo-West Pacific

These lions are known for strikingly

Antennata lionfish can be readily identified by a singular row of boldly defined eyepots on their pectoral fin webbing and their bright white fin rays.

beautiful pectoral fin rays that are long, thick, and bright white. These fish also have six prominent spots on their face and boldly defined eyespots on their fins. They are found in shallow water on reef flats and at a depth of 50 meters (160 feet) in the fore-reef zone. During the day they hide in caves, and divers report seeing as many as six specimens sharing the same hiding place. In the late afternoon and toward dusk, the lions emerge to hunt, usually taking four to six prey items.

Antennata lions are a hardy medium-sized lionfish for the home aquarium. They are beautifully marked with alternating vertical bands of reds, whites, and browns and are readily identified by their pectoral fins, which possess webbing that connects only halfway up the fin ray. This membranous area has one or more dark spots resembling eyespots. The posterior portion of each fin ray is whitish, with each ray's lowest portion extending past the caudal peduncle; each fin ray is independent and not connected by webbing. The coloration of *P. antennata* is somewhat variable; some individuals will possess bright red striping while others will have brownish red, almost resembling the *P. mombassae* lion. These two fishes are frequently misidentified and lumped together as "antennata lions."

Although it feeds primarily on crustaceans in the wild, the antennata lionfish will readily consume live fish, including any tankmates small enough. They do prefer shrimp over fish and are readily established on ghost shrimp and then weaned onto prepared foods like frozen *Mysis* or whole krill.

At first these lionfish are shy and will spend a lot of their initial time in the tank hiding. If you are keeping more than one, make sure that each has its own hiding spot. It is best to provide more caves than necessary to prevent squabbling over prime sites.

Pterois mombasae

Common Names: African lionfish, deepwater firefish, devil lionfish, frill fin turkeyfish, Mombasa lionfish.
Size: 8 inches (20 cm)

Mombassa lionfish are deepwater fish that can be identified by the multiple rows of eye spots on the pectoral fin webbing.

Distribution: Indo-West Pacific, from South Africa to Sri Lanka and New Guinea

This deepwater lion is frequently confused with the antennata lion, since it has similar pectoral fins and body color patterns, but the Mombasa lion can be identified by its numerous eyespot bands on the pectoral fins and its blurry banding pattern.

This is not a common lionfish, even in the wild. It is usually found on muddy bottoms about 50 meters (160 feet) deep, often in association with sponges. Its rarity and deepwater habitat make it harder to find in the trade and relatively more expensive. If properly acclimated, however, it makes an excellent aquarium specimen. Husbandry and care for this lion is exactly the same as for *P. antennata*.

Pterois radiata

Common Names: Clearfin lionfish, clearfin turkeyfish, radial firefish, radiata lion, scorpion radiata.
Size: 9–10 inches (23–25 cm)
Distribution: Indo-West Pacific, from Durban in South Africa and Red Sea to India, Sri Lanka, and New Guinea.

The radiata lion is easily identified by its bold and chameleon-like colorations: various shades of red with green and black overtones, separated by shocking white stripes. The characteristic two horizontal stripes on the caudal peduncle have identified this species. Radiata lions are found at depths to 15 meters (50 feet) and are usually seen around coral heads, on reef flats, and in shallow lagoons. During the day this lionfish spends most of its time hiding in crevices, under rock ledges, and in caves. Although it is primarily a solitary fish, two or three radiata lions have been observed sharing the same cave. At dusk these fish move onto the reef flats, where they fully extend their fins and begin their hunt. During their hunting they assume a unique posture—they tilt forward, pectoral fins extended, head slightly down. According to Michaels (Michaels, 1998) this fish feeds exclusively on crabs. It is also reported, however, to eat shrimp. Like other lionfishes, radiata lions prefer to eat many smaller items over ingesting a single larger one.

In my experience this species ships poorly, so finding a good healthy specimen can be difficult. These lions are also considered rare in the wild are therefore not frequently seen in the lionfish trade, and they subsequently command a higher price. I consider them to be among the more beautiful lionfish, as the markings and patterns on them are so variable that they are almost chameleon-like. The body markings consist of alternating wide vertical bands of dark red, browns, black-reds, red-greens, all separated by a sharp white stripe. The caudal peduncle has two bands that point

toward the tail fin. The second dorsal as well as the anal and caudal fins are clear and without spots or markings. The pectoral fins are spectacular white rays with membranous webbing only on the bottom quarter. When these lionfish swim they extend their pectoral fins, accentuating the white stripe pattern.

Radiata lions are uncommon in the hobby and often fail to acclimate to captivity. They often insist on eating only live shrimp and crabs.

In the home aquarium, this species is one of the more difficult lionfish to keep, for a number of reasons. First, they often arrive at the fish stores in poor condition. Second, they are passive and do not compete well for food against tankmates. Third, they are intolerant of poor water quality and often succumb to illness as water quality declines. Fourth, I have found these lions to prefer to eat shrimp and crabs over fish, and I've had to establish them using ghost shrimp and small fiddler crabs as first foods. Once they are established on these foods, however, it is difficult to wean them over to prepared foods. With special care and patience they will eventually accept other foods and will ultimately survive quite well in the home aquarium.

Parapterois heterura

Common Names: Blackfoot firefish, bluefin firefish, bluefin lion, gurnard lionfish, threadtail firefish.
Size: 9 inches (23 cm)
Distribution: Indo-West Pacific, from east Africa to southern Japan.
  This bottom-dwelling lionfish is marked similarly in coloration to *D. zebra* except

Bluefin lionfish are new to the aquarium hobby, and little is known about its captivity husbandry. So far this fish has proven difficult to keep. Specimens from tropical populations may fare better.

that the axillary side (inner surface) of the pectoral fins is solid black with neon fluorescent-blue flashes. The bluefin lion is unique in that it possesses elongated upper caudal fin rays that extend well past the tail. It has a truncate (squared off) caudal fin and two dermal appendages that extend past its lower lip, similar to what is seen in *D. biocellatus*. Thus this fish appears to be a fusion of a Fu Man Chu lionfish head with the body of a dwarf zebra lion in shape and coloration. The beautiful blue broken bands on the axillary side of the pectoral fins are not visible when the animal is resting, as the fins are kept close to the body, but when it gets excited it rapidly extends its fins, displaying a black surface with flashing neon-blue stripes. This is truly an amazing visual display. First the fish rears up from its pit and extends its dorsal spines towards the attacker. Next, it flicks its pectoral fins and rotates its body 360 degrees.

Found in temperate waters to 300 meters (1000 feet) deep, this is a unique lionfish in that it remains hidden in the substrate; during the day it is frequently found half buried in a silty or sandy pit that it excavates. Additionally, the fish will remain in open reef flats and coastal bays, in fine sand or muddy habitats and in zones of clear sandy bottoms, with minimal hiding areas. At dusk it is more active, hunting for small fish and crustaceans. This is a rare and elusive fish; most specimens are observed from trawls by commercial fishing vessels on muddy bottoms at depths over 40 meters (130 feet). There are no reports about its diet or its social organization.

This is a new introduction in the marine hobby, and therefore we have very limited hands-on husbandry information. The primary reason why it hadn't been collected for trade is its requirement for cool water. In 2005, a few shipments of bluefin lions collected from the Philippines were brought into the USA, and from these limited fish a number of hobbyists provided anecdotal reports. Essentially, the husbandry for this fish is the same as for mid-sized lionfishes, with the two major additions of including sandy substrate and cool water. In the home aquarium the bluefin lionfish will find an appropriate site and begun to excavate a shallow depression; once the pit is created the lionfish will hunker down within it. Initially they require live foods, but a number of hobbyists report being unable to wean these fish onto prepared marine foods.

To date there have been no hobbyist reports of successful long-term keeping of these fish. Of the few hobbyists who have had success getting them to eat prepared foods, no reports suggest they were able to keep the fish longer than a year, and most perished within three months of purchase. The reasons why this fish is proving to be so difficult to keep are unclear. Since its initial description this lionfish has been considered to be a temperate-water fish; its collection from the Philippines suggested that a warm water-tolerant population was being collected, but dive reports indicate that individuals are located in the areas of coolest water, near coldwater upwellings. Still, hobbyists using temperate tank setups with chillers also reported their bluefin lionfish perished within a few months. The collection of these fish could also be responsible for its shortened life span, as many collection stations are not set up to handle temperate-water fish. All fish are placed into tropical water, and this may unduly stress them. This phenomenon is also observed in the temperate-water Catalina goby, *Lythrypnus dali*, a small colorful goby found off Catalina Island, where collection and holding occurs under tropical water conditions and shortens

Pterois andover has only recently been discovered in the waters off Halmahera. It seems to prefer areas with sandy or muddy bottoms.

the life span of the fish even if they are subsequently kept at the right temperature. Whatever the case may be, bluefin lionfish do poorly in the home aquarium. While spectacular, they cannot be recommended for the home aquarium until more is learned about their specific needs.

Large Lionfishes

The large lionfishes are extremely popular aquarium specimens, and with good reason. They have many attributes that make them hardy and interesting pets. Unfortunately, they are also extremely commonly mistreated to the point of early death. The leading causes of their demise are being kept in too small an aquarium (with the resultant poor water quality issues) and being fed a steady diet of live goldfish. Keep and feed them properly and they will be beautiful, hardy, and long-lived (seven to ten years).

Pterois andover

Common Names: None yet.

Size: 12 inches (30 cm), taken from approximation in dive photographs. Juvenile specimens collected so far have ranged from 8.3 to 16.9 cm (3 to 6½ inches).

Distribution: Western Pacific: Indonesia and New Guinea.

This is a newly described (2008) lionfish family member identified by six specimens collected at southwest Halmahera, Papua New Guinea. This lionfish is rarely seen due to its inclination toward turbid inshore reefs possessing soft sand-mud bottoms. Individuals superficially resemble small *P. volitans* but differ in having larger body scales and usually 13 pectoral fin rays (versus 14 on *P. volitans*). The two species are readily distinguished on the basis of dorsal fin morphology, particularly the shape and color of the spine membranes—*P. andover* possesses a narrow membrane posteriorly on each spine, which is a uniform brown and terminates in an exaggerated pennant-like structure. In contrast, the membranes of *P. volitans* are broader and boldly striped, and they usually lack a well-defined terminal pennant. The new species also has consistently fewer and fainter spots on the caudal, soft dorsal, and soft portion of the anal fin. This lionfish has not entered the aquarium trade yet, but it's a very attractive and potentially hardy lionfish.

Pterois miles

Common Names: Devil firefish, Indian turkeyfish, solider lionfish.

Size: 14 inches (35 cm)

Distribution: Indian Ocean and the Red Sea, also known in the eastern Mediterranean. Recently established as an invasive alien species in the Atlantic Ocean along the eastern seacoast to Bermuda and Cuba.

    P. miles is a coastal species that is frequently observed in mud flats and silty waters. This fish differs from *P. volitans* in having numerous close-set tubercles along the cheek (Michael, 1998). Additionally, it is slightly smaller than *P. volitans* and lacks two dorsal spines and one anal spine. At the pet store you will be hard pressed to tell these two species apart. The good news is that the husbandry for *P. miles* is identical to that for *P. volitans*. Many hobbyists have maintained *P. miles* lionfish for many years thinking they were *P. volitans*.

Pterois russelii

Common Names: Clearfin lionfish, largetail turkeyfish, lionfish, plaintail lionfish, plaintail turkeyfish, planetail firefish, red volitans, Russel's firefish, Russel's lionfish, spotless butterfly cod, spotless firefish, zebrafish.

Size: 12 inches (30 cm)

Distribution: Widespread in the Indo-Pacific.

    Russel's lions are one of the more commonly available lionfishes in the hobby and are frequently called "red volitans." This

P. miles is extremely similar to the more common *P. volitans*. *P. miles* never has more than 10 dorsal spines, a detail that may be hard to see on a moving fish.

Often called the red volitans, Russel's lionfish is similar to the volitans but Russel's has no spots on the second dorsal, caudal, or anal fins.

fish has a body shape and striping pattern similar to those of *P. miles* and *P. volitans*, but their coloration is more white than brown. Additionally, all their accessory fins are transparent and devoid of any spotting or marking. Russel's lionfish are found in coastal South African waters near silty mud flats and estuaries. Dive reports suggest it's a commonly found species in shallow water, but the fish has also been photographed by submersibles at depths over 100 meters (300 feet). There are few data on what *P. russelii* feeds on in the wild, but in its common range there are plentiful crabs, shrimp, and fish.

Juveniles have a whitish body with dark brown vertical stripes. As the animal ages, the body pattern becomes more diffuse and turns rust-brown in color, while the pectoral fins turn darker. The second dorsal as well as the anal and caudal fins are clear, with an occasional brown spot. The head features two pointed supraocular projections and a few lower tassels that hang off the mandible.

As aquarium residents, Russel's lions adapt easily and quickly to aquarium life. They almost always wean to prepared foods, only requiring a few days of starvation to entice them to eat a wiggling silverside or chunk of krill, and they pose no issues in competing successfully for food. Russel's lions spend almost all their time out in the open and will often swim boldly with other tankmates in search of food. They never harass tankmates, except midsized fish that appear to be potential food. Once the lion establishes that it can't eat them, they are left alone. I have found these fish to grow fairly quickly when fed properly, and they will easily become 10 inches long within one year.

Pterois volitans

Common Names: Butterfly cod, common lionfish, featherfins, firefish, lion fish, lionfish, ornate butterfly cod, peacock lionfish, red firefish, red lionfish, scorpion volitans, scorpion cod, turkey fish, turkeyfish, volitans lion, and zebrafish.

Size: 17 inches (43 cm)

Distribution: Throughout the Pacific Ocean. Recently established in the Atlantic Ocean along the eastern seacoast to Bermuda and Cuba.

For many people this is *the* lionfish. The most common lionfish in the hobby, the volitans is a hardy species great for a large aquarium. The coloration is both variable and attractive. These fish are generally sold in two color morphs: a red form with reddish/brown stripes and a black morph with black markings. The amount of black or red varies with the collection locale of these fish, and even solid black specimens make their way into stores. A Red Sea population has been collected in which the regular pointed supraocular tentacles have evolved into beautiful feather-like structures.

Juveniles have wonderful busy vertical stripes alternating with lighter and white outlines. The pectoral fins are disproportionately long; each ray is individually webbed, and the center of the pectoral fin is frequently clear. As these lionfish age, they appear to separate into two categories; while the striped body pattern becomes more diffuse, in

The volitans lion is highly variable in color. This is a nicely marked red individual.

A population of volitans lionfish in the Red Sea has feather-like appendages over the eyes.

one group the pectoral fins appear to shorten, resulting in a squatty large-bodied fish with short fins, whereas the other group of lionfish also is squatty and large-bodied but retains proportionally longer fins.

There is considerable confusion between *P. volitans* and *P. miles*. It has been suggested that *P. miles* is restricted to the eastern Indian Ocean and the Red Sea, whereas *P. volitans* is restricted to more western waters (Schultz, 1986). The only physical differences between the species are two additional dorsal spines and one additional anal spine in *P. volitans* and that *P. miles* is smaller.

In the home aquarium volitans lions make beautiful and interesting centerpiece fish. Frequently offered for sale as 2-inch (5-cm) juveniles, they are cute and adorable, with tremendous personality. Juveniles are active swimmers and are constantly searching out food. These fish almost always wean over to prepared food quite well, usually with no more assistance required than adding shrimp or fish chunks to the water column. They are aggressive feeders and will actively compete with fast-swimming fish like tangs and wrasses. The main problem is their size; the cute juvenile at the store will reach 8 to 10 inches (20 to 25 cm) in one year's time with proper feedings and good water quality and within six more months it will attain a size of 15 inches (40 cm) or more. These fish easily outgrow their tankmates and eat them. Any fish that is half the body size of the lion is considered food and will be eaten eventually. These fish also have a very large pectoral fin span and therefore require a large aquarium, and even though they tend to be more sedentary as adults, they still need to turn around, so a tank 18 inches (45 cm) from front to back is the minimum. Collection reports on the Atlantic *P. volitans* lionfish confirm that they are outgrowing their Pacific Ocean counterparts, with numerous 17-inch (43-cm) long individuals being collected. Since the Atlantic population seems to be enjoying a relatively predator-free environment, this would indicate that captive specimens can reach larger sizes as well.

This is a bold, top-tier predator in the reef, frequently observed hovering above the fore-reef in clear view. In the wild they spend dawn/dusk periods in open water in search of foods (primarily fish), and frequently travel in packs of five or more animals. During the daylight hours they head to cave openings and protected structures such as reef ledges and shipwrecks for safety.

Adults feed primarily on fish; however, they have been observed engulfing crabs and shrimp as well. Juveniles appear to eat more invertebrates than fish. An interesting observation about their hunting techniques is that they will drag their lower pectoral fin tips through the mud and silty substrates in hopes of stirring or surprising a hidden fish or crab. They have also been observed hunting in packs in which the group of lionfish will herd potential prey items into a tight pack and alternate turns engulfing them. A dive report suggests that they also will follow larger foraging predators and pick off the scurrying fish trying to escape.

It can be difficult to determine the species of juvenile lionfish because they have not developed adult colors and fins. This may be a young Russel's lion.

Species Guide: Scorpionfishes

In this chapter we'll look at the Scorpaeninae—scorpaenid species that are usually called scorpionfishes. They all have large heads, oversized mouths, and large eyes. They possess rigid spines on the dorsal, anal, and pelvic fins that are associated with venom-producing tissues or glands, and are capable of delivering a potent wallop when injected. The toxicity of scorpionfish venom varies from species to species, and the composition and volume injected dictate the overall effects.

Scorpionfish are mostly solitary in nature. When multiple specimens of the same species are housed together, they usually will fight.

In the wild scorpionfish are found on living on all surfaces, from sandy, muddy, soft bottoms to rocky outcrops and coral rubble. They spend their days lying in wait for passing food, both in darkened areas such as in crevices, underneath outcrops, and in the shadows, or with some species in the open. To ensure their invisibility, scorpionfish blend into their surrounding by possessing muted colors, cryptic patterns, and dermal appendages, and some species even allow filamentous algae and cyanobacteria to grow on their skin. Although some scorpionfishes may actively lure food items into range, most rely on concealment to ambush unsuspecting prey. The diet of reef-living scorpionfishes varies, with a few larger species feeding primarily on fish and smaller species eating crustaceans. However, scorpionfish will generally eat any animal small enough to swallow that passes within range. Like their cousins the lionfish, scorpionfish tend to be crepuscular, feeding primarily at dusk, when they will ingest one or two food items and then retire to digest their capture.

The Scorpion Tank

Scorpionfishes generally make great aquarium specimens. There are hardy and good-natured, and they don't bother anyone that won't fit into their mouths. Since they are very sedentary and spend much of their time immobile, waiting for food, they don't need huge tanks. Their hefty appetites and large waste production, however, make them unsuitable for small tanks. I have seen very nice scorpionfish setups containing one or two small specimens—under 4 inches (10 cm)—in a 20-gallon (80-liter) long tank. A standard 55-gallon aquarium would work suitably for several medium-sized scorpionfish, and maybe even a dwarf lionfish or two. For any scorpionfish aquarium, ensure that you have robust biological and mechanical filtration, and be consistent in the water quality control. Frequent water changes using buffered seawater should accompany regular monitoring for climbing nitrates and pH drop.

Aquascaping

You should provide areas of rocky surface and rubble to *Parascopaena* and *Sebastapistes*, who prefer to hide in caves and underneath rock overhangs, whereas *Scorpaenopsis* prefers open areas. I recommend a sandy substrate instead of crushed coral, which requires regular vacuuming sessions to eliminate any detritus accumulation.

Like their lionfish cousins, scorpionfish are technically reef safe but also reef limiting. Aside from the unwelcome heavy bioload they present, you also obviously have to skip the ornamental shrimp and crabs as well as small fish. And while these fishes don't prey on corals, a scorpionfish might rest on a large coral during the day, eventually killing it.

Feeding

As with lionfish, you will most likely have to initiate feeding using live ghost shrimp. I've had a few scorpionfishes over the years prove difficult to downright impossible to wean onto prepared food, but by using the techniques I described you should be able to get most of them to eat non-living foods.

While scorpionfish (*Scorpaenopsis oxycephala* here) are not usually aggressive to tankmates, they will eat anything that can fit in their cavernous mouths.

Tankmates

Scorpionfish are generally solitary animals. Avoid buying multiples of the same species unless you know they won't fight or have an extremely large tank. Fighting in scorpionfish initiates with visual displays such as opening of their mouths, flaring of the gill covers, and extending of the fins towards the rival. If the opposing fish doesn't retreat, the threatening scorpionfish will resort to head-biting its rivals. If you observe the fight escalating, remove the offending fish. Fighting happens more frequently in smaller tanks where territories cannot be established, or if a new scorpionfish is added to a tank already containing one. On the other hand, scorpionfishes usually don't have a problem with other scorpionfish species, and I've never witnessed a scorpionfish harassing any non-conspecific tankmate—unless it was trying to eat it.

Scorpaena brasiliensis

Common Names: barbfish, orange scorpionfish
Size: 9 inch (23 cm)
Distribution: Western Atlantic and Gulf of Mexico, North Carolina to Brazil.

This scorpionfish inhabits coral reefs, rubble, and sandy zones where it's frequently found hidden in clumps of algae. It ranges down to 100 meters (325 feet). In the wild it feed primarily on crustaceans, such as shrimp and crabs, but in the home aquarium it will eat anything. Provide it with plenty of hiding spots and macroalgae if you want to observe it in a natural environment. This is a very common scorpionfish that you will see in the pet store, as it's very attractive and surprisingly active. Its reddish-orange body with two small devilish horn-like supraocular projections makes the fish an eyecatcher. The species is incredibly hardy and will feed on everything from ghost shrimp to your prized pygmy angels, so consider its tankmates wisely.

The orange scorpionfish is one of the most commonly available species. It's also extremely hardy and good choice for a first scorpionfish.

Scorpaena plumieri

Common Names: Lion fish, Pacific spotted scorpionfish, plumed scorpionfish, prickly hind, spotted scorpionfish, stinging grouper.
Maximum size: 18 inches (45 cm)
Distribution: Coastal US from Massachusetts, through Gulf of Mexico to southern Brazil and east to Africa.

The spotted scorpionfish is found in shallow water primarily on coral reefs and rubble patches, frequently hiding on or near small rocky outcrops. The fish will frequently reside on reef flats, and it is common to observe it lying on the open sand near rockwork. Juvenile fish are prevalently found in heavy seagrass and algae zones. In the wild, this fish feeds primarily on fish, but it has been observed eating crabs and shrimp. In the home aquarium plumed scorpionfish are hardy.

Scorpaena plumieri hiding in plain sight off the coast of Honduras.

S. plumieri can be readily identified by the three dark bands on its tail. I have seen this species at the pet stores in browns, grays, and light mottling over a gray-red body color—it's a very attractive scorpionfish. The inner surfaces of its pectoral fins possess flasher colors that are exposed when the animal feels threatened. Additionally, this fish has numerous mandibular dermal flaps that appear beard-like and camouflage the face, head, and chin. Although it gets fairly large, it's not boisterous or problematic. If the filtration system can handle it, the spotted scorpionfish also makes an interesting reef tank dweller, as it tends to sit out in open areas, away from your corals. However, due to its size you must make certain its tankmates are bigger than this fish. Observations in the wild indicate that this scorpionfish will even ambush tangs and wrasses.

Parascorpaena mossambica

Common Names: Golden scorpionfish, Mozambique scorpionfish.
Size: 4 inches (10 cm)
Distribution: Widespread throughout the Indo-Pacific.

This is a diminutive scorpionfish that is found in lagoons, reef flats, and channels in relatively shallow water. It is frequently located in rubble zones, where it spends much

As with lionfishes, it is important that you can identify a scorpionfish you are considering to know what its mature size will be. Unfortunately, just identifying the genus will not do the trick with scorpionfishes, as there is considerable variation in size even within a genus. If you still have doubts after comparing a fish to the descriptions and photos in this book, do more research before acquiring a new specimen.

of its time hiding underneath overhangs and in crevices. To identify this species, look for two large hooked-forward tentacles over its eyes. In the home aquarium, these little scorpionfish make interesting pets, as they frequently will huddle near rockwork, but still in full view. I recommend you aquascape starting with sandy substrate, a few open areas, and rock rubble to provide plenty of caves, crevices, and overhangs. Because of its smaller size, you will have to initiate feeding using small ghost shrimp or feeder guppies, but they do wean readily onto prepared foods. This is a scorpionfish that will do well in a nano tank of 12 to 20 gallons (45 to 75 liters).

Scorpaenodes caribbaeus

Common Name: Reef scorpionfish.
Size: 5 inches (12 cm)
Distribution: Florida and the Bahamas and Caribbean islands south to Panama to northern South America.

This is a very common species that is found everywhere from tidal pools to reef slopes and fore-reef zones. It is frequently observed sitting on hard surfaces and rubble and associated with sponges. It often spends its day inverted on the ceiling of caves or ledges and has been reported to eat small shrimp and crabs. You can identify this species easily because it has spotted pectoral, dorsal, and caudal fins; additionally, the face and cheeks are spot-covered. This fish appears smooth and lacks tassel adornments. Juvenile fish have two colored bands on their pectoral fins and a faint band on the caudal peduncle. Similar to the Mozambique scorpionfish, this diminutive scorpionfish requires a sandy substrate and rock rubble to create plenty of hiding spots, caves, and rock overhangs. Be aware that these fish tend to be less aggressive feeders than most other scorpaenids, so consider mellower, slow-feeding tankmates.

Scorpaenodes parvipinnis

Common Names: Coral scorpionfish, lowfin scorpionfish, shortfinned scorpionfish, shortspined scorpionfish.
Size: 5½ inches (14 cm)
Distribution: Widespread throughout the Indo-Pacific.

The lowfin scorpionfish inhabits areas of rich coral growth from near shore to the outer reef slopes in relatively shallow water. It is found associated with sponges and patch reefs and hidden among encrusting invertebrates on man-made

One of the smaller scorpion species, the lowfin scorpionfish is suitable for reef tanks as long as you are careful not to house it with fish large enough to eat it.

structures, and it's reported to feed exclusively on small shrimp. You can identify it by noting a broad whitish saddle-like marking on the middle portion of the body. Although this fish has a highly variable coloration, most specimens you'll see for sale will be pinkish or gray and possess many small skin flaps. They also have an extremely short dorsal fin. I recommend aquascaping the tank with a sandy substrate and numerous rubble outcroppings. Providing plenty of hiding spots and caves makes the fish feel at home. Due to its small size, it will also do quite well in a reef tank; however, don't expect to see it until the lights go out.

My lowfin scorpionfish readily ate small ghost shrimp and small damsels, but I was unable to wean this fish onto prepared foods.

The devil scorpionfish often has algae growing on its skin enhancing its already excellent camouflage.

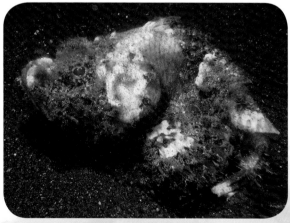

Scorpaenopsis diabolus

Common Names: Devil scorpionfish, false scorpionfish, false stonefish.
Size: 12 inches (30 cm)
Distribution: Widespread throughout the Indo-Pacific.

The devil scorpionfish is

Bearded scorpionfish are enthusiastic eaters, and it usually is not difficult to wean them onto prepared foods.

an uncommonly seen fish that inhabits rubble or weedy coralline rock bottoms of reef flats and lagoon and seaward reefs. It is found in both shallow water reef flats and deeper water on sandy slopes. It prefers protected habitats such as rock outcropping and heavy algal growth. Its color is highly variable, ranging from pink to gray, and frequently a fish is found with filamentous algae growing on its skin, which further enhances its camouflage. I have seen a number of juvenile specimens at the local pet stores colored blotchy purple and appearing as if they were covered with coralline algae. *S. diabolus* is a member of the humpback scorpionfish species, along with *S. gibbosa* and *S. macrochir*. All humpback scorpionfishes possess a hump on the middle of the back that gives them a rounded appearance. They also they possess flasher colors on the inside of their pectoral fins that get exposed when the fish swims.

In the home aquarium humpback scorpionfish are easy to keep. They feed readily on live foods, especially small live feeder fish, but they have proven difficult to wean onto prepared items. They have excessively large mouths and can easily swallow all but the largest of their tankmates, so choose accordingly. As is so often the case with scorpions, *S. diabolus* makes a good reef tank specimen, as it will sit out in the open away from your corals for extended periods, but it is reef limiting with that big mouth and hearty appetite.

Scorpaenopsis barbata

Common Names: Bearded scorpionfish, tasseled scorpionfish.
Size: 9 inches (22 cm)
Distribution: Western Indian Ocean, Red Sea to at least the coast of Somalia.

S. barbata is in the tasseled scorpionfish group, along with *S. cacopsis, S. oxycephala, S. papuensis,* and *S. venosa*, whose heads and lower jaws possess a number of dermal fringes and tassels that give the fish a bearded or fuzzy look. Most of these species are associated with hard substrates and coral fringes, spending the day perched on rocks or coral rubble or hiding among soft corals like *Sarcophyton* and *Xenia*.

These are attractive fishes, with colors ranging from rusty red to mottled brown, and many of them appear heavily speckled and fuzzy. Many related species in this group all look the same to the untrained eye, so differentiating them will be all but impossible. The good news is that the husbandry is the same for all of them.

Aquascape with sandy substrate and provide multiple patches of rock rubble, as these fish tend to sit out in the open on top of the rockwork. Initiate feeding using ghost shrimp or feeder fish; I find bearded scorpionfish to eat so ravenously that they readily accept prepared foods within a few weeks. A few hobbyist reports suggest they also have limited color-changing ability, in which brightly appearing individuals can turn dark and vice versa, so when aquascaping, consider providing a few differently colored zones, as it may result in some unique-looking fish.

Sebastapistes cyanostigma

Common Names: coral scorpionfish, yellowspotted scorpionfish.

Size: 4 inches (10 cm)

Distribution: Widespread throughout the Indo-Pacific.

The yellowspotted scorpionfish is a hard coral dweller that limits its range to within a coral colony. Typically found among the branches of *Pocillopora* corals in surge areas of seaward reefs, as well as between the branches of corals such as *Stylophora* and *the* fire coral, *Millepora*. All feeding occurs on fish and invertebrates that live among the coral

The yellowspotted scorpionfish is another small species suitable for reef tanks. Provide coral branches or coral rubble for this species to dart among as it would in nature.

branches. These are attractive little scorpionfish that frequently show up with yellow pectoral fins and yellow spotting on a reddish brown body color. They appear to possess oversized eyes and aren't as sedentary as many other scorpionfish. In the home aquarium, it is best to provide this fish with a sandy substrate, some rock rubble, and either live or dead pieces of *Pocillopora* skeletons. It will frequently take up residence among or on top of the coral branches, awaiting any passing fish or invertebrate for food. These fish feed aggressively on ghost shrimp and any small feeder fish, but I was never able to get them to eat prepared foods, so ensure that you have a constant access to live foods when considering this species. Other hobbyists have reported that their yellowspotted scorpionfish did eventually take frozen foods, so perseverance is required. Since these fish are so small, they can be kept with bigger fish in a mid-sized reef tank or as a centerpiece for a nano tank.

Variability

Scorpionfishes are a diverse group and vary considerably in size, coloration, habitat, behavior, and diet. Many of them are very difficult to wean off live foods. Make sure your setup is suitable for a fish before bringing it home, and unless you have seen it feed on prepared foods—always a good idea—be prepared to provide live foods on a long-term if not permanent basis.

Other Scorpionfishes: *Pteroidichthys*

Some scorpionfishes are rare, both in the wild and in the hobby, and they tend to be quite different from most other Scorpaeninae. The first of these is the Ambon lionfish.

Pteroidichthys amboinensis

Common Names: Ambon lion, Ambon scorpionfish.
Size: 5 inches (12 cm)
Distribution: Indo-West Pacific: known from disjunct localities. Red Sea, Indonesia, Papua New Guinea, Japan, and Saipan; known only from five specimens taken from the Ryukyu Islands, Celebes, Ambon, Viet Nam, and Madras.

Ambon scorpionfish look and act much like *Rhinopias*—part fish, part living algae clump. The Ambon lion is a master of camouflage. Found primarily along soft-bottom habitats or in algae patches in shallow water up to 180 meters (600 feet) deep, Ambon lions are a rare sighting. Dive reports suggest that these fish can be found in the open near a lone piece of detritus or algae. Additionally, when they are sighted they are seen in pairs and trios in which one individual is considerably larger, suggesting potential sexual dimorphism. The coloration of Ambon lions varies according to their surrounding environment; everything from golden yellow to browns, and green to reds, has been photographed. A distinguishing feature of Ambon lions is their supraorbital tentacles; these horn-like dermal extensions above the eyes can resemble rabbit ears to multi-pointed caribou antlers and everything in between. The fish have fairly smooth faces but possess a mustache-like dermal tassel frequently rimmed with hair-like extensions. In addition, the level and amount of Ambon lions' camouflage varies depending upon where they are found. For example, Ambon lions located in open areas can be relatively smooth but lightly decorated in small hair-like threads, whereas Ambon lions found associated with filamentous algae beds frequently possess more dermal tassels and hair-like extensions. The pectoral fins, which are usually held at 45- or 90-degree angles from the body, are used to stabilize the animal as it crutches forward on its pelvic fins. Additionally, the pectoral fins tend to have a lacy quality, almost window pane-like, as these features disrupt the fish's silhouette when viewed from the front.

Ambon lions are a wonderful little fish for a species-only or slow-moving, slow-feeding tank. They are the closest fish that many of us will ever get to keeping a *Rhinopias* in that they act like and appear very similar to weedy *Rhinopias*. Ambon lions are very slow-moving fish that stealthily crutch their way across the bottom, but when harassed they can hop quickly forward. Pairs and trios of these fish appear to get along and in larger tanks they prefer to remain together. As for feeding, Ambon lions prefer live ghost shrimp and small feeder guppies; I was never able to get these fish to wean onto prepared foods, so make sure you have access to live foods before

Ambon lionfish are slow-moving and somewhat fragile fish. They should not be kept with fast-moving, quick-feeding fish, or they will not be able to obtain food.

considering purchasing an Ambon lion. Additionally, slow-feeding and slow-moving tankmates are required, as Ambon lions are just not competitive feeders. One report suggests that male Ambon lionfish are "larger," possess larger heads, and have more dermal flaps; while this may be true, these subtle differences are difficult to assess, as these fish seldom appear at the pet store. If you're able to acquire a pair of Ambon lions you may be rewarded with frequent spawnings in which the larger fish (presumably the male) will court the female during the evening period; should the female be gravid, the pair will perform an abbreviated spawning session, resulting in an egg mass that quickly disperses through the tank. I have been fortunate to keep a number of these fish over the past few years, and while they appeared healthy and well fed, they would succumb for no obvious reasons after around three to six months. Other anecdotal reports from fellow hobbyist have suggested the same in that the fish, while initially taking food and doing well, appear fragile long-term. Therefore I can only recommend *P. amboinensis* for intermediate to advanced hobbyists who can dedicate a species-only tank to keeping these marvelous little fish.

Other Scorpionfishes: *Rhinopias*

The genus *Rhinopias* contains eight species, of which only three are seen in the hobby with regularity. These fish were considered rare until the past few years, were infrequently collected for anything but public aquariums, and cost thousands of dollars. However, their rareness was apparently due to their distribution in regions that were infrequently used as collection sites. Currently I see them on many wholesaler lists and at my local fish stores, at somewhat affordable prices. The good news is that hobbyists can now keep these incredible scorpionfishes and the hobby will learn a great deal about their husbandry. The bad news is that if these fish are truly rare, then the current level of collection may be unsustainable. No juvenile *Rhinopias* have been reported in the wild, suggesting both a cryptic nature and a relatively low reproduction rate. Obviously more study is needed.

All *Rhinopias* have a strongly compressed body with eyes set high on the head, and the head is thinner than the body width. The pelvic and pectoral fins are used to crutch along with an occasional speedy hop toward food items. Rarely do these fish swim. Three species, *R. eschmeyeri*, *R. frondosa*, and *R. aphanes*, are similar to each other in overall body appearance, and most of their morphometric and meristic characters overlap. In addition, they share the following characters: one or two small dense black spots approximately equal in size with pupil diameter, in the middle of the membrane between the sixth and ninth dorsal soft rays. The first few rays of their dorsal fin form a sail, and in *R. frondosa* and *R. eschmeyeri* the fin membranes can be used to differentiate them—*R. eschmeyeri* possesses a flat sail, but in *R. frondosa*

Pink variety of the weedy scorpionfish. This species usually does well in captivity, feeding on damsels and saltwater minnows.

its appears like a jagged ridge. The heads and faces of both species are adorned with multiple dermal appendages: supraocular projections appearing like antlers, spikes or algae fronds, and mandibular and maxillary projections appearing like mustaches, plant fronds, or hair algae.

Telling Them Apart

The eye tentacles are very useful characters for distinguishing these species. *R. eschmeyeri* can easily be distinguished from *R. frondosa* and *R. aphanes* by its lack of tentacles on the frontal region below the eyes, compared to two pairs of tentacles in *R. frondosa* and one or two pairs in *R. aphanes*. Additionally, tentacles on the head and body in *R. eschmeyeri* and *R. frondosa* are fleshy and thickened compared to those in *R. aphanes*. The dorsal fin spines also show differences. *R. eschmeyeri* and *R. frondosa* have relatively soft spines tips that easily bend under slight pressure. In contrast, *R. aphanes* has spines typical of most scorpionfishes: they are firm, with strongly pointed tips.

In addition to the above-mentioned morphological characters, the three species can be distinguished by their body pattern. While coloration in *R. eschmeyeri* shows considerable variation among individuals, the entire head, body, and fins are a single uniform color, devoid of pattern. *R. frondosa* and *R. aphanes* are heavily patterned. *R. frondosa* individuals possess body patterns that appear as elongate ocelli or circular markings, while *R. aphanes* possess complex maze-like body markings. These diverse body patterns suggest to taxonomists functionality in the camouflage of the fish. *R .aphanes* is thought to mimic a noxious-tasting crinoid (feather starfish), and *R. frondosa* is thought to be an algae mimic. Both species are covered with dermal tags and body adornments. *R. eschmeyeri* is the plainest looking of the three, lacking many of the body adornments and having only a pair of tentacles on the lower jaw, and two small supraocular tentacles.

One Species or Two?

Some scientists consider *R. frondosa* and *R. eschmeyeri* one species. Michael (1998) has observed pairs of *Rhinopias* in which two individuals looked totally different, one appearing to be *R. frondosa* and the other *R. eschmeyeri*, implying that this difference may be sexual dimorphism. To counter this, a recent investigation argues that there are two valid species here and cites a paper (Motomura, 2006) in which expanded gonads full of well-developed eggs were confirmed in specimens from both types, suggesting that there are male and female animals of both. Taxonomists work mainly with preserved animals, but there is a potential for a fish to undergo a morphological change in captivity. This feature has been observed in a number of antennarids (anglerfishes) that undergo severe color changes when removed from the wild and kept in the home aquarium. An anecdotal report from Hemdal notes that he has witnessed

Yellow variety of *R. eschmeyeri*. These fish rock their bodies in the current, mimicking a clump of algae.

Lionfishes and Other Scorpionfishes

a long-term captive *frondosa* type morph into a fish resembling an *eschmeyeri* type. Unfortunately, DNA evidence has yet to resolve this issue. This species or these species are the species most commonly available, and *R. aphanes* is rarely imported—if you do see one for sale, expect a few more final zeros on the price tag.

Husbandry Notes

The proper care of the rarer scorpionfishes in this section is similar to that of other Scorpaeninae. They are very sedentary fishes and are perfect for smaller display tanks that can highlight one fish. I have seen a number of *Rhinopias* displayed in a long tank subdivided into smaller display chambers. These fish make good tankmates in that they have no interest in other fish they can't fit into their mouths. Do not, however, house them with aggressive tankmates or tankmates that tend to forage on rocks, as they may mistake the scorpionfish's skin for algae. I have seen a number of beautiful reef tanks containing *Rhinopias*, though, of course, this requires skipping ornamental shrimp or crabs and any small fish. My personal recommendation is to keep one of these rarities in a display tank by itself. I wouldn't risk one with any other fish. Aquascaping can include a sandy substrate with rockpiles and cave structures, clumps of macroalgae, and suitable open areas. In the wild, these fish will sit in open zones and gently rock, mimicking wave action on a plant.

They rarely swim, but when fed they will quickly hop toward their prey. One hobbyist reported that her fish would pace the tank when hungry and immediately hop toward the food once it hit the tank. Initially many find that live small damsels, saltwater "minnows," or mollies are needed to stimulate feeding, with many specimens refusing live ghost shrimp. Some hobbyists report that their fish never wean onto prepared foods.

Many specimens frequently shed their cuticle. In some individuals this shedding can occur quite frequently—every 12 days. One hobbyist reported his scorpionfish would often face into the outflow of the return pump to assist in removing the cuticle being shed. *Rhinopias* species appear susceptible to marine ich and velvet, but they can be sensitive to copper-based medications.

Rhinopias have been displayed in public aquaria for many years and have been considered to be short-lived species with survival rates averaging two to three years. With an increasing number of hobbyists now keeping *Rhinopias*, reports are beginning to suggest successful long-term survival of these fish greater than three years. It will be interesting to see how long these fish actually do live in the home aquarium.

R. aphanes is rare in the aquarium hobby and seems to be rare in nature as well. This one was photographed off Papua New Guinea.

Rhinopias aphanes

Common Names: Lacy scorpionfish, Merlet's scorpionfish, weedy scorpionfish.
Size: 10 inches (25 cm)
Distribution: Only in the Coral Sea area.

This is the largest of the three *Rhinopias* and is found on coral slopes, rocky substrates, and soft bottom habitats, frequently associated with masses of living crinoids. This fish appears site-specific, frequently located in the same region for several months. The common color phase for this fish is yellowish, with elongate black-margined markings; however, red to white, brown to black, and lilac to purple specimens have been photographed. They are covered with numerous filamentous tentacles appearing like algae on the lower jaw and body. The pectoral fins are resplendent with alternating areas of clear membrane and color.

This fish is reported to be quite hardy and tolerant of tankmates as well as being a good feeder. I've only seen two specimens, and both fed well on live ghost shrimp and damsels. These fish are very rare in the wild and carry a very hefty price tag when they are available. If you can find this fish and can afford it, it's the ultimate scorpionfish.

Rhinopias eschmeyeri

Common Names: Eschmeyer's rhinopias, Eschmeyer's scorpionfish.

Size: 6½ inches (17 cm)

Distribution: Indo-West Pacific.

This species occurs in deep reefs, lagoons, and on external reef slopes on open sand or rubble bottoms. It lies in ambush close to coral outcrops, rubble piles, and algae tufts. It has been photographed in yellow to pink, brown to red, and light blue to purple. One photograph suggests that mottled individuals may also exist.

In the home aquarium *R. eschmeyeri* individuals make excellent tank inhabitants; they feed well, they are tolerant of many larger fish, and they are quite hardy. For aquascaping, these fish require little more than sand or crushed coral substrate, a few pieces of rock to crawl over and open areas to sit. These *Rhinopias* can thrive well in a reef-tank setup, as they crawl among your rockwork and when hungry become more obvious. When keeping *Rhinopias eschmeyeri* in reef tanks, be sure its tankmates won't end up as food and, importantly, make sure your *Rhinopias* gets adequately fed. Many fast-swimming fish will outcompete these slow-moving predators for floating food. My experience with them is that, while sedentary, they tend to become more active as they become hungrier. In addition, I noted that each fish had a few quirky mannerisms, such as only hopping to catch prey versus crutching on their fins. These fish would also rock back and forth, mimicking wave action on algae. One hobbyist reported her *R. eschmeyeri* would kick sand up using its tail fin whenever tank maintenance would occur even though he was on the opposite side of the tank. Many hobbyists keep *Rhinopias* with larger less aggressive fish, like large lionfish or tangs, with few compatibility issues. In regard to feeding, I've not found an individual *Rhinopias* that would not stalk live fish, so I recommend that you initiate feeding using live saltwater feeder fish, such as damsels or small sheepshead minnows; smaller fish appear more enticing than larger ones. Many hobbyists keeping these fish report feeding their *Rhinopias* live feeder fish their entire captive lives; however, they will eventually wean onto prepared foods.

Rising Stars

The hobby is seeing an increase in the number of *Rhinopias* being offered for sale. Although still somewhat pricey, they are appearing more and more often in more variety, and more hobbyists than ever are fulfilling their dream of owning one of these exotic animals.

Rhinopias frondosa

Common Names: Popeyed scorpionfish, weedy scorpionfish.

Size: 9 inches (23 cm)

Distribution: Indo-West Pacific.

This fish resides in rich soft-bottom habitats, near rocky areas intermixed with algae, where it feeds upon small fish and invertebrates. Many of the specimens arriving at the pet stores are being collected from Sri Lanka. It has complex body markings of repeated ocelli and multiple dermal appendages that give the fish its "weedy" appearance.

In the home aquarium, weedy scorpionfish make excellent tankmates; they feed well, are tolerant of many larger fish, and are quite hardy. To initiate feeding, I recommend the use of live saltwater feeder fish, such as damsels or sheepshead minnows, eventually training the scorpionfish onto prepared foods. I would feed three to four times weekly, but many hobbyists find it easiest to feed *ad libitum* (as they wish), meaning that they provide a few damsels in the tank at the beginning of the week and allow the fish to eat at its own pace. Once most of the feeder fish have disappeared, they restock the food supply. If you do utilize the "as they wish" feedings, ensure that the feeder fish are being fed a nutritious marine-based food while they are in the *Rhinopias* tank and ensure also that the feeder fish are not harassing the *Rhinopias*. As for aquascaping and compatibility, everything that was said about keeping *R. eschmeyeri* applies here.

Rarer Scorpions: *Taenianotus*

The scorpaenid species *Taenianotus triacanthus* is called a "leaf scorpionfish." That same common name is applied also to some fishes in the subfamily Choridactylinae (usually lumped under the name "stingfishes") of the family Synanceiidae, which we'll cover in the next chapter.

Taenianotus triacanthus

Common Names: Leaf fish, leaffish, leaf scorpionfish, paper fish, paper scorpionfish, paperfish, sailfin leaf fish, sailfin leaffish, swayfish, three-spined scorpionfish, threespine scorpionfish.

Size: 4 inches (10 cm)

Distribution: Throughout Indo-Pacific.

The genus *Taenianotus* contains this single species, which is common in the hobby. Leaf scorpionfish inhabit reef flats, outer reef slopes, current-swept channels, and lagoon reefs. This fish is solitary and usually found among algae, seagrass, coral branches, and rubble. They are seen sometimes in pairs, though, and they do not seem to be bothered by the presence of one or more conspecifics in close proximity. They feed on small crustaceans and small fish, including fish larvae. The body is laterally compressed, with a high dorsal fin, which makes them appear like a blade of algae.

They have evolved two unique movements that further the illusion

Spectacular pink leaf scorpionfish in a coral reef off Sulawesi, Indonesia. These fish are hardy in the aquarium when kept with other slow-moving, nonaggressive tankmates.

that they are nothing but plant debris; one movement mimics the swaying of algae fronds or leaf blades in the current, as the fish will rock from side to side. The second movement involves a hip roll that resembles that of a leaf falling through the water. They are found in a variety of colors ranging from brown and black to pink, white, yellow, and red, and they possess the ability to lighten and darken their colorations.

Leaf scorpionfish are a wonderful little fish for a small species tank or a low-stress tank containing slow-feeding mellow tankmates. They are the slowest-feeding scorpionfish you'll ever see. Over the years I've kept many of these fish and never observed any aggressive behavior among them. I did notice that leaf scorpionfish shed their cuticle frequently, approximately two times per month, starting from the head region first.

For a scorpionfish *T. triacanthus* has a very small mouth and eats proportionally small food items. All of mine ate only small live ghost shrimp and feeder guppies, though I was eventually able to wean just one over to frozen mysis.

Species Guide: The Odd, Unusual, and Amazing

There are several other scorpaeniforms that can be considered for the home aquarium, mostly in the family Synanceiidae. The fishes of one group, however, should never be considered for purchase.

Stonefish conceal themselves among rocks or under the sand where they may be stepped on by unfortunate swimmers. Stonefish stings are usually lethal.

A Scorpaeniform to Avoid

Stonefishes, species in the subfamily Synanceiinae of the family Synanceiidae, are the most venomous fishes in the world. People are usually envenomated when they step on a concealed fish, and they usually die. While all the other fish covered in this book are venomous and warrant extremely careful handling, their stings are not generally lethal. Stonefish, on the other hand, have no place in the aquarium hobby.

Aquatic Cobras

The venom of stonefish is equal in toxicity to that of a cobra. Each dorsal fin ray possesses two grooves that facilitate venom flow. Even the smallest juveniles have fully developed venom glands and spines that can inflict excruciating pain and serious tissue damage to an adult human being. As such, any stonefish is considered a lethal risk and does not belong in any home aquarium.

Stonefishes in the Hobby

Given what I just told you about the lethal nature of stonefish venom, you may be surprised to hear that these animals are found for sale fairly often. There are seven species in the genus *Synanceia*, but only one, *S. verrucosa*, is seen much in the hobby. Usually called the reef or common stonefish, it grows to 14 inches (36 cm).

This is the most widespread stonefish in nature, ranging throughout the Indo-Pacific. It is found on sandy and rubble areas of reef flats, in shallow lagoons, and in shallow pools. It sits near coral and reef rubble, under rock ledges, or semi-buried in soft sand or mud. The fish is incredibly well camouflaged, with colors that can vary from black to dark brown, rust, and yellow. Additionally, stonefish in general have the ability to adjust their pigmentation depending on the colors of substrate and are frequently decorated with orange and yellow pigment patches that mimic sponges or coralline algae, further camouflaging them. Stonefish are unbelievably sedentary and may remain unmoving in the same spot for days.

These animals adjust very well to captivity and have an ugliness that appeals to many people. They are easy to wean onto prepared foods and will eat practically anything. They can eat other fish their own size, including other stonefish. So yes, the stonefish is easy to care for, but it remains completely motionless for hours at a time, can be difficult to see in its half-buried, camouflaged state, and cannot be kept with most other fishes. Top that off with the fact that one careless move on your part when caring for it or servicing its aquarium, and you're dead!

Don't misunderstand me. These are interesting fish, but the dangers they pose clearly outweigh any reason to keep them. They are fish that should be enjoyed at your local public aquarium. Otherwise, enjoy a photo of a stonefish, not the real thing.

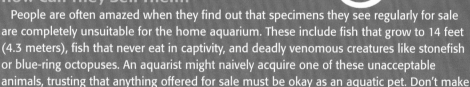

How Can They Sell Them?

People are often amazed when they find out that specimens they see regularly for sale are completely unsuitable for the home aquarium. These include fish that grow to 14 feet (4.3 meters), fish that never eat in captivity, and deadly venomous creatures like stonefish or blue-ring octopuses. An aquarist might naively acquire one of these unacceptable animals, trusting that anything offered for sale must be okay as an aquatic pet. Don't make this mistake—research any animal before buying it!

Stingfishes

The family Synanceiidae does have some aquarium potentials, however, in the subfamily Choridactylinae— the genera *Inimicus* and *Choridactylus*, generally known as stingfishes, sea goblins, or bearded ghouls. While not usually lethal, these close relatives of stonefish have a very potent sting

Bearded ghouls frequently bury themselves, so a sandy substrate is recommended for a tank housing these odd fish.

and pack a painful wallop. Their sting should not be treated lightly—people have died as a result of their venom. So, as with all other scorpaeniforms, be aware at all times when handling or maintaining these fish.

This is one of those groups of fishes that are called by a multitude of overlapping names, with some people distinguishing one species from another by a common name that other people use for the other species. Be aware that you absolutely cannot rely on common names to identify these fishes.

Choridactylines have two or three free pectoral rays that are not connected to the rest of the pectoral fins. These rays are curved downward and can move independently like fingers to propel the fish as it scurries over substrate. *Inimicus* species appear to walk clumsily as they drag their strongly curved tails behind them. In *Choridactylus* the fingers are also used to forage through the sediment to locate and dig up buried food items. The second common feature in Choridactylinae is the presence of flasher coloration on the inner surface of the pectoral fins. When startled the fish spread their pectoral fins, rotating them forward to expose the bright coloration.

The various stingfishes make interesting and downright weird aquarium residents. The tank bottom should have a few inches of sand or finely crushed substrate, as these fish spend a lot of time partially buried. It's not uncommon to see only exposed eyes and mouth or a half-buried head.

Tankmates are problematic. Almost any other fish will outcompete them for food, and many will try to snack on the skin adornments that make the stingfish look like sponges, rocks, and algae.

My *C. multibarbus* only ate small ghost shrimp, never anything else. I was unsuccessful at weaning them onto anything prepared. The *Inimicus* were slightly better, however; they preferred live ghost shrimp but would also take guppies. Over a four-month period I was able to wean these fish onto frozen mysid shrimp, and then prepared seafood chunks.

Choridactylus multibarbus

Common Names: Bearded ghoul, many-barbed stingfish, orange stonefish, orangebanded stingfish, stonefish.

Size: 5 to 6 inches (14 cm)

Distribution: Indo-West Pacific, from the Red Sea and the Persian Gulf eastward to Pakistan, India, Thailand, China, and the Philippines.

This is the only one of the four species in this genus ever to be seen in the hobby. Apparently a tasty fish, it is sold in Asian markets either fresh or salted and dried. However, most specimens collected for the hobby come from the Philippines, where the fish is found inhabiting sandy or muddy bottoms. It is one of those fish that some find downright ugly while others find it appealing. Color ranges from solid gold to mottled brown and gray and even to those highly prized specimens that are covered in pink, red, and coralline algae-like patches. The fins are frequently a different color from the body, and this species always has a dark band on the base of its tail. The head is rounded and the eyes set wide apart. Dangling from the lower jaw are multiple tassels or fringes—its "beard."

I found these fish hardy, tolerant of tankmates, and good eaters, as long as the live ghost shrimp kept coming. (A few hobbyists have reported successfully weaning their ghouls over to prepared foods.) These fish clumsily crawl over rockwork, so be aware if you keep this species with loose corals or have tenuously stacked rocks. They also spend a good portion of their waking hours digging and partially burying themselves, so a sandy substrate is recommended. And remember, these fish have rigid dorsal spines that can deliver a very potent sting, far greater than you'd expect from a fish this size.

Genus *Inimicus*

These fish inhabit sandy and muddy bottoms in sea grass fields, estuaries, and neighboring reefs. Although *Inimicus* species prefer shallower water, there are records locating them in as deep as 90 meters (300 feet). There are about ten species, of which three are found with any regularity in the hobby. *Inimicus* differs from *Choridactylus* by its flattened snout, eyes set high on the head, and two free pectoral fin rays that are used as fingers. In Japan, *Inimicus* are cultured as a delicacy food, and induced ovulation using hormones to increase production has been reported (Takusima, 2003).

Like the other choridactylines, these stingfish spend their day half buried or mostly buried in the soft sand, with only their eyes, dorsal fins, and mouth exposed. Individuals frequently have their two free pectoral fin rays placed ahead of the body and dug into the substrate in case a food item zips by; the fish can then spring into pursuit. Some species have even higher-set eyes and an upturned mouth that allows the fish to bury themselves more completely to really surprise passing food. In the wild they eat mainly fish, but they readily take live shrimp.

Inimicus are some of my most favorite scorpions. I have kept fishes of this genus on and off for 10 years. Each of them had a distinct personality and very interesting hunting behaviors. Their strategies include an ambush attack from underneath the sand, a relativity fast stalking using the pectoral fingers to scamper quickly to the food, and a pounce from above. They readily fed on live ghost shrimp and small feeder guppies, and I successfully weaned them onto prepared foods, although it did take longer than I had hoped. These fish spend their day buried with just their eyes sticking out of the sand, and they spring to life when food hits the water. It is reported that *Inimicus* kept in groups will fight, but they

Sea goblin (*I. caladonicus*) photographed in the waters off Sulawesi, Indonesia. These fish dwell mostly in muddy- or sandy-bottomed water and seagrass beds.

never bother tankmates too large to swallow. Mine were hardy and disease resistant, ate consistently, and shed their cuticles with regularity. Another reminder: they pack a very potent sting, stronger than a lionfish sting.

Inimicus caladonicus

Common Names: Bearded ghoul, Caledonian sea goblin, Caledonian stinger, Chinese ghoul, demon stinger, demon stingerfish.

Size: 10 inches (25 cm)

Distribution: Eastern Indian Ocean: Andaman and Nicobar Islands; West Pacific: Australia, Papua New Guinea, and New Caledonia.

   This fish is very similar to *I. didactylus* but differs in the coloration of its pectoral fins, in which the inner surface contains a dark band that runs through the middle and a dark band on the inner axial of the fin. Additionally, Caledonian sea goblins frequently have white spots in front of their elevated but wide set eyes.

Inimicus didactylus

Common Names: Bearded ghoul, demon stinger, devil stinger, longsnout stinger, longsnout stingerfish, popeyed sea goblin, spiny devilfish.

Size: 10 inches (25 cm)

Distribution: Indo-West Pacific: Thailand to Vanuatu, north to Ryukyu Islands and southeast China.

   I. didactylus makes a fine aquarium resident. It requires at least 2 inches of fine sand or sandy substrate. In my experience this fish frequently comes in with amazing colorations—such as yellow, red, and white. The red variants look like living piles of red sponge with encrusting algae. Gray fish tend to have uniquely colored pectoral

Inimicus didactylus flaring out its brightly colored pectoral fins in a territorial display.

fins. *I. didactylus* differs from its congeners in the undersides of its pectoral fins: a sweeping yellow or white band with a darkened half-moon center. It also has a slightly upturned mouth.

Inimicus filamentosus

Common Names: Barred ghoul, devil scorpionfish, filamented sea goblin, filament-finned stinger, two-stick stingfish.
Size: 10 inches (25 cm)
Distribution: Western Indian Ocean: the Red Sea and East Africa to the Maldives.

I. filamentosus showing the eye-catching pattern on its pectoral fins. This fish was photographed in the Red Sea near the Sinai Peninsula.

The filamented sea goblin appears to be an advanced form of *Inimicus*, as it has both an upturned mouth and high-set fused eyes, allowing it to almost completely bury itself and still efficiently ambush unsuspecting food. The species can be readily identified from other *Inimicus* by the presence of two extended filaments on the pectoral rays, and by the yellow, red flasher colors on the underside of its pectoral fins. I have not seen this fish in many other body colors except dull grayish brown, with pinkish overtones; however, Fishbase.org has an image of a reddish pink specimen. This fish is quite uncommon at pet stores. Care and husbandry is the same as the other *Inimicus* species, if you can find it.

Waspfishes

Once included in Scorpaenidae, subfamily Tetraroginae, the waspfishes are now considered a separate scorpaeniform family, Tetrarogidae. Features that exclude them from Scorpaenidae include a dorsal fin that originates above and in front of the eyes, in contrast to the scorpionfishes, in which the dorsal fin originates well behind the eyes. Waspfishes have contiguous-appearing dorsal, caudal, and anal fins, whereas scorpionfishes have those three fins separate. Waspfishes also possess small scales embedded into their skins, and they are more laterally compressed than typical scorpionfish (except the leaf scorpionfish). Taxonomic considerations aside, waspfish look like scorpionfish, act like scorpionfish, carry venom like scorpionfish, and require the same care as scorpionfish.

Of the many genera and species in this family, only three species (in two genera) are seen in the hobby with any regularity. These animals are wonderful aquarium specimens. Besides being relatively small, they are also extremely sedentary and spend most of their day in one spot or slowly hopping along the bottom in search of food. Always ensure that your waspfish's tankmates do not out-compete them for food and do not pick on them as food items.

These fish blend well into dark substrates and piles of live rock. Aiding their external camouflage is their habit of slowly rocking side to side as if they are algae swaying in the current.

Waspfish are incredibly slow feeders and cannot be placed in a tank with any fast-swimming fish. I found them difficult to feed and only got them to eat live ghost shrimp; they had little interest in feeder guppies. Eventually I was able to wean them onto prepared frozen mysis shrimp; however, they always preferred live food.

The basic husbandry requirement for all the species of waspfish appears to be the same. They prefer a mellow community tank, with slow-feeding neighbors. Good tankmates would include: small scorpionfish, leaffish, and smaller antennarids (anglerfish). The tank can be aquascaped with small piles of live rock or rubble that include a few hiding spots, or even containing live macroalgae for the fish to hide in during the day. I've kept up to three waspfish in the same 30-gallon (115-liter) tank with no visible fighting, and as mentioned in the breeding section, I was able to get these fish to spawn.

Ablabys macracanthus

Common Names: Spiny leaf fish, spiny waspfish.

Size: 8 inches (20 cm)

Distribution: Indo-West Pacific.

This species is less commonly available than *A. taenianotus* but does show up occasionally. The dorsal fin crest starts ahead of the eyes, making it slant backward down to the face, while in *A. taenianotus* it is nearly vertical.

Ablabys taenianotus

Common Names: Cockatoo fish, cockatoo leaf-fish, cockatoo waspfish, leaf fish, rogue fish, roque fish, rouge fish.

Size: 6 inches (15 cm)

Distribution: Eastern Indian Ocean and Western Pacific

This is the more common species seen in pet stores. Individuals are varied in coloration, ranging from dark brown to golden, but usually are a solid color. Reportedly female cockatoo waspfish have single white spots or blotches above and below their lateral lines on both sides of their body, while males lack spots above the lateral line. Also male cockatoo waspfish are reported to have one or two white spots on the distal edge of their gill opercula, while females do not.

Paracentropogon longispinus

Common Names: Long-spined waspfish, whiteface roguefish, Whiteface waspfish, wispy waspfish.

Size: 5 inches (13 cm)

Although no longer considered to be in the same family as the scorpionfish, the waspfish are very similar in appearance, behavior, and care. *A. taenianotus* is shown here.

The long-spined waspfish is the species most often found in the aquarium hobby. It is an extremely slow feeder and strongly prefers live over prepared food.

Distribution: Indo-West Pacific: southern India to southern China and New Caledonia.

This waspfish looks more like a scorpionfish, with a dorsal fin that starts directly above the eyes. This is the only species in this genus that I have seen for sale. While coloration is said to be extremely varied, ranging from solid brown to rust red to pink and white, every specimen I've encountered was solid brown, with a white rectangle on the face.

Conclusion

You now have a good foundation for enjoying scorpaeniform fishes in your own aquaria, and you've had an overview of most of the species you will find for sale in the aquarium hobby. I've incorporated my more than 20 years of hands-on experience keeping these fishes into this book and shared with you, the reader, useful tips and techniques to help you succeed with them. I hope you will consider rising to the challenge of breeding these fishes in your tanks, and I wish you luck in discovering the secrets to successfully rearing the fry of these magnificent animals.

References

Auerbach, PS, McKinney HE, Rees RS, Heggers JP. Analysis of vesicle fluid following the sting of the lionfish *Pterois volitans*. *Toxicon* **25** (1987): 350–351.

Cameron, AM, Endean R, Epidermal secretions and the evolution of venom glands in fishes. *Toxicon* 11 (1973): 401–410.

Chan, TY, Tam LS, Chan LY, Stonefish sting: an occupational hazard in Hong Kong. *Ann. Trop. Med. Parasitol.* (1996), (90):675–676.

Chen D, Kini RM, Yuen R, Khoo HE, Haemolytic activity of stonustoxin from stonefish venom: pore formation and the role of cationic amino acid residues. *Biochem. J.* (1997) 3254:685-91.

Church JE, Hodgson WC, Adrenergic and cholinergic activity contributes to the cardiovascular effects of lionfish (Pterios volitans) venom. *Toxicon*, (2002) **40**:787-96.

Cohen AS, Olek AJ, An extract of lionfish (*Pterois volitans*) spine tissue contains acetylcholine and a toxin that affects neuromuscular transmission. *Toxicon* **27** (1989): 1367–1376.

Cuvier, G, Le Règne Animal, distribué d'après son organisation, pour servir de base à l'histoire naturelle des animaux et d'introduction à l'anatomie comparée. Edition 2., Règne Animal (Ed. 2), (1829)2:1-532.

Fenner, PJ. Marine envenomation: an update—a presentation on the current status of marine envenomation first aid and medical treatments. *Emerg. Med.* (2000), 12: 295–302.

Fishelson L. 1975. Ethology and reproduction of pteroid fishes found in the Gulf of Aqaba (Red Sea), especially *Dendrochirus brachypterus* (Cuvier), (Pteroidae, Teleostei). PSZN 39 (Suppl. 1):635-656.

Fishelson L, Oogenesis and spawn-formation in the pygmy lionfish *Dendrochrius brachypterus*. *Marine Biology*, 46, 341-48, 1978.

Fishelson L, Experiments and Observations of Food Consumption, Growth and Starvation in *Dendrochirus* and *Pterois*, *Env. Biol Fish*, (1997) **50**:391-403.

Garyfallou GT, Madden JF, Lionfish envenomation. *Ann Emerg Med* **28** (1996), pp. 456–457.

Green SJ, Cote IM, Record Densities of Indo-Pacific Lionfish on Bahamian Coral reefs, *J. Int Soc. Reef Studies*. Abstract.

Grobecker DB, "The lie-in-wait" feeding mode of a cryptic teleost, *Synanceia Verrucosa*, *Env. Biol. Fish*, (1983)**8**(3/4):191-202.

Gwee MC, Gopaalakrishnakone P, Yuen R, Khoo HE, Low KS, A Review of Stonefish Venom and toxins, *Pharm. Ther.* (1994), **64**:509-28.

Hamner RM, Freshwater DSW, Whitfield PE, Mitochondrial cytochrome b analysis reveals two invasive lionfish species with strong founder effects in the western Atlantic, *J. Fish Biol.* (2007) **71**:214022.

Hemdal, J. *Advanced Marine Aquarium Techniques*, TFH publications, USA. 2006.

Khoo HE, Yuen R., Poh CH., Tan CH., Biological Activities of *Synanceia horrida* (Stonefish) venom. *Nat. Toxins.* (1992), (**1**):54–60

Khoo HE, Bioactive proteins from Stonefish venom, *Clinical and Expt. Pharm. Physiol.* (2002) 29:802-6.

Kizer KW, McKinney HE, and Auerbach PS., Scorpaenidae envenomation: a five-year poison center experience. *JAMA* (1985), **8**:807–810.

Koya Y, Munoz M., Comparative study on Ovarian structures in Scopaenidae: Possible evolutional process of reproductive mode. *Ichthy. Res.* (2007), **54**(3):221-30.

Imamura, H, Shinohara, G, 1998. Scorpaeniform fish phylogeny: an overview. *Bull. Nat. Sci. Mus., Ser.* A 24, 185–212.

Imamura H, Yabe M, Demise of the Scorpaeniformes (Actinopterygii: Percomorpha): an alternative phylogenetic hypothesis. *Bull. Fish. Sci.,* Hokkaido Univ. (2002) 53, 107–128.

Karpestam J, Gustafsson J, Shashar J, Katzie G, Kroger RHH, Multifocal Lenses in coral reef Fish, *J. Expt Biol.* (2007) 210:2923-31.

Maretic Z, Fish venoms. In: *Handbook of Natural Toxins: Marine Toxins and Venoms,* Marcel Dekker, AT Tu, Editor New York (1988), pp. 445–477.

Michael, SM. *Reef Fish, Vol1,* TFH Microcosm, USA 1998.

Motomura H, Johnson JW, Validity of poorly known scorpionfish, *Rhinopias eschmeyeri,* with a redescription of *R. frondosa* and *R. aphanes. Copeia,* (2006) 3:500-15.

Patel MR, Wells S, Lionfish envenomation of the hand. *J. Hand Surg.* 18 (1993), pp. 523–525.

Ruiz-Carus R, Matheson RE, Jr., Roberts DE, Jr., Whitfield PE. The western Pacific red lionfish, *Pterois volitans* (Scorpaenidae), in Florida: Evidence for reproduction and parasitism in the first exotic marine fish established in state waters. *Biological Conservation.* (2006) **128**:384-390.

Russell FE, Toxic effects of animal's toxins. In: C.D. Klaasen, Editor, Casarett and Doull's *Toxicology—The Basic Science of Poisons,* McGraw-Hill, Sydney (1996).

Sauviat MP, Meunier FA, Dreger A, Molgo J, Effects of trachynilysin, a protein isolated from stonefish (*Synanceia trachynis*) venom, on frog atrial heart muscle. *Toxicon* (2000), **38**: 945–959

Schaeffer RC, Carlson RW, Russell FE, Some chemical properties of the venom of the scorpionfish *Scorpaena guttata. Toxicon* 9 (1971), pp. 69–78.

Schaper A, Desel H, Ebbecke M, de Haro L, Deters M, Hentschel H, Hermanns-Clausen M, Langer C. Bites and stings by exotic pets in Europe: An 11-year analysis of 404 cases from Northeastern Germany and Southeastern France. *Clin Toxicol* (Phila). 2008 Apr 7:1-5.

Schultz, ET. *Pterois volitans* and *Pterois miles*: two valid species. *Copeia,* (1986):686-90.

Shinohara G, Comparative morphology and phylogeny of the suborder *Hexagrammoidei* and related taxa. *Mem. Fac. Fish.,* Hokkaido Univ. (1994) 41, 1–97.

Shiomi K, Hosaka M, Fujita S, Yamanaka H, Kikuchi T, Venoms from six species of marine fish: lethal and hemolytic activities and their neutralization by commercial stonefish antivenom. *Mar. Biol.* 103 (1989), pp. 285–289

Smith, WM Leo, Wheeler, WC, Polyphyly of the mail-cheeked fishes (Teleostei: Scorpaeniformes): evidence from mitrochondrial and nuclear sequence data. *Mol. Phylogen, and Evolution,* (2004) 32:627-46.

Sutherland SK, Tibballs J. *Australian Animals Toxins: The Creatures, their Toxins and Care of the Poisoned Patient* (Second Ed.), Oxford University Press, Melbourne (2001).

Takushima M, Nozaki R, Kadomura K, Yasumoto S, Soyano K. Induced ovulation using LHRHa and artificial fertilization in the devil stinger, *Inimicus japonicus. Fish Physiol and Biochem.* (2003) 28(4):521-22.

Thresher, RE. *Reproduction in Reef Fishes.* TFH publication Inc, Ltd. 1984.

Toonen, R., Value of Live Foods for Coral Reef Aquariums, part1- *Advanced Aquarist Online* magazine 2003. (http://www.advancedaquarist.com/issues/dec2003/invert.htm).

Trestrail, JH, Al-Mahasneh QM, Lionfish sting experiences of an inland poison center: a retrospective study of 23 cases. *Vet Hum Toxicol* **31** (1989), pp. 173–175.

Vetrano SJ, Lebowitz JB, Marcus S, Lionfish Envenomation, *J. Emerg.Med* (2002) 4:379-82.

Wasserman GS, Johnston M, Poisoning from a lionfish sting. *Vet. Hum. Toxicol.* 21 (1979), pp. 344 345.

Wittenrich ML, Lionfish: An Overview. *Seascope,* Volume 15, 1998.

Resources

Magazine & Online Forum

Tropical Fish Hobbyist
1 T.F.H. Plaza
3rd & Union Avenues
Neptune City, NJ 07753
Email: info@tfh.com
www.tfhmagazine.com

Internet Resources

Aquarium Hobbyist
www.aquariumhobbyist.com

Marine Ornamental Fish and
Invertebrate Breeders Association
www.marinebreeder.org

Microcosm Aquarium Explorer
www.microcosmaquariumexplorer.
com

Reef Central
www.reefcentral.com

TFH Forum
http://forums.tfhmagazine.com

Wet Web Media
www.wetwebmedia.com

Associations and Societies

Federation of American Aquarium
Societies (FAAS)
Email: Jbenes01@yahoo.com
www.faas.info

Marine Aquarium Societies of North
America (MASNA)
http://www.masna.org/

Books

Fenner, Robert. *The Conscientious Marine Aquarist.* Microcosm/T.F.H. Publications, Inc.

Kurtz, Jeff. *Saltwater Aquarium Problem Solver.* T.F.H. Publications, Inc.

Kurtz, Jeff with David E. Boruchowitz. *The Simple Guide to Marine Aquariums, Second Edition.* T.F.H. Publications, Inc.

Hellweg, Michael R. *Culturing Live Foods.* T.F.H. Publications, Inc.

Paletta, Michael. *The New Marine Aquarium: Step-By-Step Setup & Stocking Guide.* Microcosm/T.F.H. Publications, Inc.

Ward, Ashley. *Questions & Answers on Saltwater Aquarium Fishes.* T.F.H. Publications, Inc.

Index

Acknowledgements

I'd like to thank Carla S., Alison R., and Keri W., for graciously reviewing my manuscript many, many times, and providing so much valuable input. I am indebted to Renee Coles-Hix, Bob Fenner, Edgar Dunn, and the many photographer friends who graciously donated their incredible scorpionfish photos that illustrate this book. Lastly, thanks to my fish geek hobbyist friends around the world, who inspired me to consider writing a book that was 30 years in the making

About the author

Frank C. Marini III, PhD, born and raised in Hudson, Massachussets, is a long time fish nerd. Working as a stem cell biologist by day, Frank's passion for keeping scorpionfish and their kin has lasted more than 30 years. His scientist side affords him a unique perspective into animal behavior, and his fish nerd

side keeps him curious and motivated to find the keys to unlocking successful long-term husbandry of these remarkable fish. In 1995, Frank was credited with the first successful breeding of Banggai cardinalfish in captivity, and his writings have inspired thousands of fishkeepers to delve into marine fish breeding. For the past 15 years he has bred many species of marine fish, and accompanying this, he has moderated web forums on fish breeding and keeping aggressive and predatory fish in the home aquarium. Frank can be contacted at fcmarini.lionfish@gmail.com.

Photo Credits

Annetje (from Shutterstock): 90

Anthony Calfo: 62

Carey Rich (from Shutterstock): 116

Yue Jason Chen: 20 (bottom), 75

Renee Coles-Hix: 5, 15, 18, 20 (top left, top right), 27, 30, 31, 33, 34, 37, 41, 42, 46, 51, 61, 92, 99, 101, 102, 108, 112, front cover, and back cover (top)

Cindy Colinvitti: 8, 14, 93

Cigdem Cooper (from Shutterstock): 97

Robert H. Creigh (from Shutterstock): 56

Edgar L. Dunn: 10, 74, 76, 87, 96 (bottom), 107, 114, and back cover (bottom)

Bob Fenner: 43, 57, 68, 72, 80, 81, 95 (top), 104, 115, 118, 119

Spencer Finn (from Shutterstock): 22

Jose Gil (from Shutterstock): 64

David Haupt: 86

Matthew Herrick: 63

Randy Katz: 70

Stephan Kerkhofs (from Shutterstock): 3, 59, 91, 110

Tan Klan Khoon (from Shutterstock): back cover (center)

Jo Lin (from Shutterstock): 47

Frank C. Marini: 25, 49, 54, 84

Ron May: 66

Nautilus Media (from Shutterstock): 44

Giuseppe Nocera (from Shutterstock): 83

Photaz (from Shutterstock): 19

Christophe Rouziou (from Shutterstock): 87

Kristian Sekulic (from Shutterstock): 13

Elisei Shafer (from Shutterstock): 17

R.C.B. Shooter (from Shutterstock): 79

Asther Lau Choon Siew (from Shutterstock): 12

Sergey Skleznev (from Shutterstock):

Vasily Smirnov (from Shutterstock): 85

Dr. Dwight Smith: 26

Edwin van Wier (from Shutterstock): 1

Mark Vander Wal: 39

All other photos courtesy of TFH Archives.